DR B.R. AMBEDKAR
A STUDY IN JUST SOCIETY

DR B.R. AMBEDKAR
A STUDY IN JUST SOCIETY

JAMES MASSEY

CENTRE FOR DALIT/SUBALTERN STUDIES

MANOHAR
2003

First published 2003

Hardbound: ISBN 81-7304-523-2
Paperback: ISBN 81-7304-524-0

Published by
Ajay Kumar Jain for
Manohar Publishers & Distributors
4753/23 Ansari Road, Daryaganj
New Delhi 110 002

in association with
Centre for Dalit/Subaltern Studies,
New Delhi 110 045

Typeset by
Kohli Print
Delhi 110 051

Printed at
Lordson Publishers Pvt. Ltd.
New Delhi 110 007

Contents

Contents

Introduction

This work is an attempt to study an alternative social order envisaged by Bharat Ratna Babasaheb Dr B.R. Ambedkar. This theme, perhaps most important, runs throughout most of his writings is actually an alternative paradigm of a social order to an existing social order based upon the caste system. His alternative is an 'ideal society' or a 'casteless society', based upon the principle of justice. I have named this society as 'just society'. In the concluding chapter Dr Ambedkar's 'envisaged' just society is discussed in detail.

Closely related to the 'just society' are the other five most important themes: 'Buddha's Dhamma', 'Dalits and the Conversion', 'Christianity and Dalit Christians', 'Dalits: A Minority' and 'Framing the Constitution'. In Chapters One and Two the first two themes are discussed, which deals with the doctrinal or conceptional basis of Dr Ambedkar's 'just society'. The discussions of Chapters Three and Four deal with the victims of the existing caste based society, which specially include the various communities of the Dalits.

According to Dr Ambedkar, 'Buddha's Dhamma' was the new paradigm of life, which offered full liberation to human beings in this world. In Chapter Two on 'Dalits and the Conversion', according to Dr Ambedkar the conversion possibly was the only way which offered to the Dalits a real 'social equality'. Similarly the discussion of Chapter Three on 'Christianity and Dalit Christians' shows his belief that Christianity can be a possible means of bringing social justice to the Dalits, but Dr Ambedkar also added that it failed because of the approach of the Christian missionaries while preaching it, which was just the opposite of the approach of Jesus and his disciples. The Chapter Four on 'Dalits: A Minority' deals with the whole issue of 'Dalits Identity'. Though in Hindu-fold, yet according to Dr Ambedkar they have their own 'Independent Identity'. The discussion of Chapter Four shows that the minorities in general and the Dalits particularly for Dr Ambedkar were not only an issue, in fact the people belonging to various minorities and the protection of their rights was one of the major concerns of his life.

Chapter Five on 'Framing the Constitution', makes a very important point clear that the exercise involved in the process of framing the Constitution was not just to provide rules and regulations to govern a country, but it was actually a process of creating a mechanism to help in establishing a democratic social order or a society based upon the principle of justice. The preamble of Indian Constitution is very clear on this point. It is because, according to Dr Ambedkar 'a democracy was not a form of government, it was essentially a form of society'. Therefore the Constitution adopted on 26 January 1950, was to be the main instrument for establishing a 'just society'.

This work basically contains a discussion on the theme of 'just society' based upon the original writings of Dr B.R. Ambedkar. I have intentionally allowed Dr Ambedkar to speak for himself, therefore the readers will find many quotations throughout this work. The theme is most relevant today, therefore it is being offered to the readers with this belief that Babasaheb Dr Ambedkar's thoughts can become the basis of dealing with the current problems related to the Dalits, tribals, women, minorities and other weaker sections of the Indian society.

11 May 2003 JAMES MASSEY
New Delhi

CHAPTER 1

Buddha's Dhamma

In Search of a New Paradigm of Life

Among the numerous important questions, the most pertinent question raised by the students of Buddhism is, 'Why did Buddha take *Parivraja* (Renunciation)?' According to the traditional answer, this was because Lord Buddha 'saw a dead person, a sick person and an old person'. But according to Dr Ambedkar, 'This answer is absurd on the face of it', because Lord Buddha took *Parivraja* at the age of twenty-nine and by that time he must have come across many times the above occurrences. Therefore he says, 'It is impossible to accept the traditional explanation that this was the first time he saw them. The explanation is not plausible and does not appear to reason. But if this is not the answer to the question, what is the real answer?'[1]

The real answer to the above question can be found by looking into the early life of Lord Buddha. Lord Buddha's father, Suddhodana, was the king of Sakya State and his mother Mahamaya was the queen. They were Kshatriyas.[2] He was born in the year 563 BC and was named as Siddharth Gautama. Before his birth some learned Brahmins prophesied to his parents, 'You will have a son, and if he leads a householder's life he will become a universal monarch, and if he leaves his home and goes forth into a homeless state, and becomes a sanyasi, he will become a Buddha, a dispeller of illusions in the world.'[3]

According to Siddharth's caste duty, he had to be trained in all kinds of war affairs because as a Kshatriya, fighting was his duty. Such beliefs based upon the philosophy that 'the worker was born to serve and that in serving his master he was only fulfilling his destiny'. A number of times he saw ordinary people working on his father's land and toiling under their labour's burden. He always questioned to his friends, 'Can it be right that one man should exploit another.' Even his mother used to worry about his attitude and often reminded him, 'You have forgotten that you are a Kshatriya and fighting is your duty. The art of fighting can be learned only through hunting. . . . Hunting is a training ground for the warrior class.'[4] But Siddharth instead of listening such advice, even in his early age believed that meditation on right subjects can lead to the development of the spirit of universal love. He argued:

> When we think of living things, we begin with distinction and discrimination. We separate friends from enemies, we separate from animals we rear from human beings. We love friends and domesticated animals and we hate enemies and wild animals. This dividing line we must overcome and this we can do when we in our contemplation rise above the limitations of practical life.[5]

Siddharth after he completed twenty years of age, was initiated into the Sakya *Sangha*. At his initiation, he took a number of vows and agreed to fulfil the duties as a member of the *Sangha*, which included safeguarding the interests of the Sakyas with his body, mind and money.[6] But after becoming a member, he soon faced a serious conflict with the *Sangha*. The neighbouring State of the Sakyas was the State of the Koliyas. Both the States entered into dispute on Rohini river's water for irrigating their fields. Siddharth was twenty-eight years old, when this clash took place between the farmers of the two States and as a result many persons were injured on both the sides. Sakya State in response to this, wanted to wage a war against the Koliyas. The Army Chief of Sakyas and the majority of his people agreed with the idea of war. But Siddharth opposed this idea because the Sakyas and the Koliyas were close relatives. Therefore he said, 'It is unwise that they should destroy each other.'[7] But the Army Chief insisted that 'in war the Kshatriyas cannot make a distinction between relations and strangers. They must fight even against brothers for the sake of their Kingdom.' He further added:

> Performing sacrifices is the duty of the Brahmins, fighting is the duty of the Kshatriyas, trading is the duty of the Vaishyas and service is the duty of the Shudras. There is merit in each class performing its duty. Such is the injunction of our Shastras.

But Siddharth, while rejecting the traditional understanding of Dharma, replied:

> Dharma, as I understand, it consists in recognising that enmity does not disappear by enmity. It can be conquered by love only.[8]

Finally the Army Chief reminded Siddharth that he could not go against the decision of the majority members of the *Sangha*, otherwise he would be punished according to the rules. He had to choose from the following three alternatives:

1. To join the forces and participate in the war.
2. To consent to be hanged or exiled.
3. To allow the members of his family to be condemned to a social boycott and confiscation of their property.

After reflecting on these three alternatives, Siddharth accepted the second one, because he was very firm regarding not joining the war and he also did not want his family to suffer, because they were innocent. He said, 'I am the guilty person. Let me alone suffer for my wrong. Sentence me to death or exile whichever you like. I will willingly accept it and I promise I should not appeal to the King of the Kosalas.'[9] Siddharth had the right to appeal, but for his conviction he was willing to forgo even that right. Both the sides agreed on the point that Siddharth should undertake self-*Parivraja*. He was at that time twenty-nine years old. Everybody admired him and said that he was the blessed one, because he chose that path 'for the sake of maintaining peace on earth and goodwill towards men'. He refused to submit for war, 'but preferred to undergo voluntary punishment which involved the exchange of riches for poverty, comfort for alms, home for homelessness'.[10] Before leaving for exile, he told the Sakya subjects who wanted to go with him that 'there is no use of your following me. I have failed to settle the dispute between the Sakyas and the Koliyas. But if you create public opinion in favour of settlement you might succeed. Be, therefore, so good as to return.'[11] The people returned on his advice.

After that there were demonstrations and processions by people carrying flags with such slogan as, 'Koliyas are our brothers', 'It is wrong for a brother to fight against brother', 'Think of the exile of Siddharth Gautama'. Finally under the pressure of the people, both Sakyas and Koliyas agreed to work through dialogue in order to avoid war. Thus the threatened war ended in peace.[12] This news was brought to Siddharth after which he could have ended his *Parivrajaka*. But he decided against it, because as a result of deep reflection, he came to the following conclusions:

> The problem of war is essentially a problem of conflict. It is only a part of a larger problem.
>
> This conflict is going on not only between kings and nations, but between nobles and Brahmins, between householders, between mother and son, between father and son, between sister and brother, between companion and companion.
>
> The conflict between nations is occasional. But the conflict between classes is constant and perpetual. It is this, which is the root of all sorrow and suffering in the world.
>
> True, I left home on account of war. But I cannot go back home although the war between the Sakyas and Koliyas has ended. I see now that my problem has become wider. I have to find a solution for this problem of social conflict.[13]

Existing Paradigm of Life

Siddharth after reaching the above mentioned conclusion based upon his personal experience realized that this conflict was going on all the levels and at all the time in this world specially 'the conflict between classes is constant and perpetual', which according to him 'is the root of all sorrow in the world'. This conflict, according to Siddharth was much wider and was a 'social conflict', to stop which a solution was required. Siddharth took a definite decision to find a solution to this problem. He first examined the existing paradigms or the old-established philosophies of life, whether these offered any solution. In his search of solution, Siddharth's first stop was at Brighu ashram, where those in search of salvation were involved in penance but he was not satisfied with these.[14] Therefore he continued his search and reached at the abode of Muni Arada Kalam, under whose direction Siddharth went through the experience of *Samadhi Marg*, which was part of Sankhya philosophy. *Dhayana Marg* (Concentration of the Mind) was part of this philosophy. The process involved was very painful and Siddharth mastered it. But both the Sankhya and *Samadhi Marg* could not help him, so he left that ashram also after rejecting the way of asceticsm.[15]

But finally Siddharth reached Gaya and went into meditation under a Banyan tree for forty days. It was here through the experience of reason, investigation, concentration, equanimity, mindfulness and complete purity of mind, he reached the depth of the problem of social conflict, which actually was centred around two problems: 'The first problem was that there was suffering in the world and the second problem was how to remove this suffering and make mankind happy.'[16] Here he found the new way to deal with this twofold problem which Siddharth named as '*Samma Bodhi*' (Right Enlightenment). Siddharth Gautama after having the *Samma Bodhi* became a Buddha. Because Siddharth became a Buddha under the Banyan tree, it also came to be known as *Bodhi* tree. Prior to becoming a Buddha, Siddharth was a Bodhisattva, i.e. a person who is seeking to be a Buddha. Bodhisattva before becoming a Buddha has to pass through ten stages of experiences. While going through this tenfold life experiences, a Bodhisattva becomes one with infinity, but he still continues to be a human 'out of his great compassion for all beings'. Finally he became Dharmamegha at tenth stage. As Bodhisattva, he 'attained the infinite divine eye of a Buddha' and so Siddharth Gautama became a Buddha[17].

Lord Buddha had a number of predecessors, which included Vedic rishis, philosophers (like Kapila, the founder of Sankhya philosophy), Brahmins (like Manu) and the authors of various Upanishadic literature. Among the ancient literature produced by various rishis and philosophers, the religious literature produced by the Brahmins was most important. It was the Brahmins' philosophy which was the foundation of not only the ancient society, but continued to be the basis of the present Indian society in general. It was the structure of this society with which Lord Buddha was concerned most. The Brahmins' philosophy according to Dr Ambedkar had four theses.

The first thesis of this philosophy is that the Vedas are not only sacred texts, but these are also infallible and cannot be questioned. The second thesis is that the salvation of soul or escape from transmigration is only possible by performing the sacrifices, observances of religious rites and ceremonies and by offering gifts to the Brahmins. The third thesis of the Brahmins' philosophy is concerned with an ideal society, which actually was one of the main subjects of Buddha Dhamma. According to this thesis, the Vedas offered an ideal structure of an ideal society based upon the rules of *Chaturvarna*. Here most important point is that Vedas according to Brahmins' philosophy is infallible and their authority is without question. Therefore the structure of society offered by the *Chaturvarna* is also binding as well as unquestionable. According to Dr Ambedkar this structure of the society was based on the following five rules:[18]

The first rule was that the society should be divided into four classes: (i) Brahmins, (ii) Kshatriyas, (iii) Vaishyas and (iv) Shudras.

The second rule was that there should not be social quality among these four classes. They always will be governed by the rule of graded inequality. At the top of all will be the Brahmins, at the next level will be the Kshatriyas, followed by the Vaishyas and lowest of all will be the Shudras. This rule of graded inequality will also govern the rights and privileges of each class. The classes will claim only the rights and privileges given to them in the Shastras. It will be an offence to claim a privilege of a higher class by the lower class.

The third rule of the ideal society based upon *Chaturvarna* was the division of occupations. The occupation of the Brahmins was learning and teaching and also performing the religious observances. The occupation of Kshatriyas was fighting and trade was assigned to the Vaishyas. The Shudras were to serve the three upper classes. These occupations were fixed and classes could not trespass upon the occupation of the other without being punished.

The fourth rule of the *Chaturvarna* based society was related to the right to education which was given only to the men of first three classes. The Shudras and women belonging to all the classes were denied this right.

The fifth rule of this ideal society was related to the four stages of human life. The first stage was *Brahamcharya*, in which men were to learn and receive education. The second stage was *Grihasthashram* in which one had to live a married life. The third stage was *Vanaprastha*, i.e. experience the life of a hermit without deserting one's home and last stage was *Sanyasa*, in which one had to go in search of God and seek union with him. These stages of life were only open to the male members of first three classes.

The fourth and last thesis of Brahmins' philosophy was the doctrine of *Karma* (transmigration) of the soul from one birth to other. The soul's transmigration depended on one's deeds of the past life.

But Lord Buddha was totally opposed to the teaching of Brahmins. For him to accept the infallibility of the Vedas meant complete denial of freedom of thought. To know the truth one has to enjoy the freedom of thought. He also rejected the rituals and sacrifices. For him sacrifice in the sense of self-denial for the good of others was the real sacrifice. The other important point was the question of inequality, which was preached by Brahmins as an official doctrine. According to Dr Ambedkar, 'Brahmanism was not content with inequality. The soul of Brahminism lay in graded inequality.'[19] In the ideal society based upon the *Chaturvarna*, both Shudras and women were fully denied these human rights which included the right to education and arms, the ultimate means of achieving freedom. These were the reasons why Lord Buddha rejected the Brahmanism.[20]

New Paradigm of Life

Lord Buddha after getting a right answer to the two basic questions of humanity, 'What are the causes of suffering and unhappiness which a person undergoes and how to remove unhappiness', he was not sure if he should go forth and preach his new doctrine (namely *Samma Bodhi*) or should continue to devote himself to his personal perfection. He was also not sure if an ordinary person would understand his new doctrine because he felt it was hard to liberate oneself from the entanglement of God and Soul and to give up one's belief in rites, ceremonies and *Karma*. After much reflection on these questions and on the suggestions of Brahma Sahampati, Lord Buddha agreed to preach his doctrine to the masses. Brahma Sahampati, a divine being even announced to the world about Lord Buddha:

> Rejoice at the glad tidings. The Buddha, our Lord, has found the root of all evil and unhappiness in the world. He knows the way out. The Buddha will bring comfort to the weary and sorrow-laden. . . . In his doctrine there is love to create a longing to own those who are disowned or unowned: to the degraded there is the ennoblement ever present to raise them: to the disinherited and the downtrodden, there is equality blazing forth their path to advancement. His

doctrine is the doctrine of righteousness and his aim is to establish the Kingdom of righteousness on earth.[21]

After taking a decision to preach his new doctrine, Lord Buddha started his missionary journey and preached his first sermon at Sarnath. In his first sermon he gave the basic essence of his Dhamma. His Dhamma had nothing to do with God and Soul, life after death, nor rituals and ceremonies.

The first feature of Lord Buddha's Dhamma was concerned with human beings and their relation with other people on this earth. The second was that human beings are living in sorrow, misery and poverty. To remove these sufferings from the world is the only purpose of his Dhamma.[22] Lord Buddha in his sermon further told, 'according to his Dhamma if every person followed (1) the Path of Purity; (2) the Path of Righteousness; and (3) the Path of Virtue, it would bring about the end of all suffering'.[23] While explaining in detail,[24] the meaning of these three aspects of his Dhamma, Lord Buddha stressed on number of virtues, which included *Karuna* (loving kindness to human beings) about which he said, 'Love is not enough; what is required is *Maitri.* It is wider than love. It means fellowship not merely with human beings, but all living beings.'[25] Here is the basis of not only human solidarity, but the whole creation. What Lord Buddha preached in his first sermon he also practised and offered a model of an alternative new paradigm through the model of his *Sangha.*

Buddha continued to preach his Dhamma among people belonging to all the classes. He preached to the nobility,[26] worshippers of fire (Agnihotris),[27] Brahmins,[28] kings[29] and persons of high status.[30] His message to all of them was to 'practise good so that good may result from our actions'.[31] Lord Buddha preached Dhamma to his family members also. During a visit to his family members, his son Rahul asked for his inheritance. At that Buddha looked towards one of his followers Sariputta and said:

My son asks for his inheritance. I cannot give him perishable treasures that will bring cares and sorrows, but I can give him the inheritance of a holy life, which is a treasure that will not perish.

Then he told Rahul:

Gold and silver and jewels have I none. But if you are willing to receive spiritual treasures; and are strong to carry them and to keep them, I have plenty. My spiritual treasure is the path of righteousness. Do you desire to be admitted to the brotherhood of those who devote their life to the culture of mind seeking for the highest bliss attainable.[32]

Lord Buddha's preachings were not limited to Brahmins, Kshatriyas and Vaishyas only, he equally went with his message to the lowest persons, which included barbar,[33] sweeper,[34] untouchable,[35] vagabond,[36] robber,[37] other criminals[38] and even lepers,[39] who were considered both low and unclean. His Dhamma was also open to women. Among his first women converts were his stepmother Mahaprajapati Gautami, his wife Yashodhara and her companions;[40] and a young Dalit girl Prakrati, who belonged to the most degraded community, Chandala.[41] Lord Buddha in his message to Prakrati at the time of her conversion said:

Blessed are thou, Prakrati, for though you are a Chandalika, you will be a model for noblemen and noblewomen. You are of low caste, but Brahmins will learn a lesson from you. Swerve not from the path of justice and righteousness and you will outshine the royal glory of queens on the throne.[42]

Prakrati after receiving the message of Lord Buddha accepted his Dhamma and later though she belonged to the lowest class, yet was admitted into the *Bhikkhuni Sangha*.[43]

Lord Buddha introduced rules for those who became *Bhikkhus* and would remain celibate. The *Bhikkhus* were organized into a *Sangha* and followed specific rules. For women, he introduced the *Bhikkhuni Sangha*. The lay followers of Lord Buddha were known as *Upasakas*. The *Upasakas* as householders had to follow strictly these rules of life particularly in relation to worldly riches and wealth:

1. The first is to acquire wealth lawfully.
2. The second is to see that their relatives also get their wealth lawfully.
3. The third is to live long and reach a great age.

According to the Dhamma, 'For a true householder for the attainment of these three things, which in the world are welcome, pleasant, agreeable, but hard to gain, there are also four conditions precedent. They are the blessing of faith, the blessing of virtuous conduct, the blessing of liberality and the blessing of wisdom.'[44] There were rules of life for children, students, husbands, wives, masters and servants also.[45]

On the other hand, the *Bhikkhus* followed a number of rules[46] and also took vows which included: vows to remain celibate, not to commit theft, not to boast, kill or take a life. It also included vows not to own anything except what the rules allowed.[47]

The *Sangha* was governed by the following rules of discipline: the *Sangha* was open to all, there was no caste, sex or status bar. Social status, caste had no place in the *Sangha*. Inside the *Sangha* all were equal and their rank was regulated by worth and not by birth.[48] Equality and equal treatment were cardinal rules for the members. Buddha himself voluntarily and willingly accepted the same rules of discipline to be binding on him also.[49]

Summary

What is Dhamma? The answer to this basic question has following six components:

1. Dhamma is to maintain 'purity of life', according to which 'one abstains from taking life, from stealing, from wrong practice in sensual lusts'.[50]

2. Dhamma is to reach 'perfection in life', which includes 'Perfection in body, speech and mind'.[51]
3. Dhamma is to live in *Nibbana*,[52] which means 'release from passion'. *Nibbana* demands a person to live righteous life which is its goal as well as its end.[53]
4. Dhamma is to give up craving. In this regard Lord Buddha said, 'that contentment is the highest form of wealth is that man should not allow himself to be overpowered by greed which has no limits'.[54]
5. Dhamma is to believe that all compound things are impermanent. The moral of his doctrine is: one should not get attached to anything, which means one should cultivate detachment from property, friends, etc., since 'All these are impermanent'.[55]
6. Dhamma is to believe that *Karma* is the instrument of moral order and has nothing to do with the fortune or misfortune of an individual. The Law of Karma is to maintain the moral order in the universe.[56]

Next important question is: *What is not Dhamma*?[57] The answer to this question has eight components:

1. Belief in the supernatural is not Dhamma.
2. Belief in *Ishwara* (God) is not an essential part of Dhamma.
3. Dhamma based on union with Brahma is a false Dhamma.
4. Belief in soul is not Dhamma.
5. Belief in sacrifices is not Dhamma.
6. Belief based on speculation is not Dhamma.
7. Reading books of Dhamma is not Dhamma.
8. Belief in the infallibility of books of Dhamma is not Dhamma.

Finally, Dhamma is also Saddhamma, which has two functions: (i) to cleanse the mind of its impurities and (ii) to make the world a kingdom of Righteouness. But Dhamma becomes Saddhamma, when it promotes three things: *Pradnya* (knowledge), *Maitri* (fellow feeling), and it must pull down all social barriers.[58] Therefore, Dhamma to be Saddhamma must

(i) Promote *Pradnya*, because Dhamma is Saddhamma when it makes education open to all; teaches that mere learning is not enough; and that what is needed is *Pradnya.*

(ii) Promote *Maitri*, because Dhamma is Saddhamma only when it teaches that mere *Pradnya* is not enough. It must be accompanied by *Sila* (moral temperament or fear of doing wrong). Dhamma is Saddhamma only when it teaches that besides *Pradnya* and *Sila*, what is necessary is *Karuna* (loving kindness) and that more than *Karuna* what is necessary is *Maitri.*

(iii) Pulls down all social barriers, because Dhamma to be Saddhamma must breakdown barriers between humans; teach that worth and not birth is the measure of human being and promote equality.[59]

In a nutshell new Dhamma or the new paradigm of life tells that 'the doctrine of a salvation is to be found here, in this life, in inward change of heart to be brought about by the practice of self-culture and self-control'.[60]

NOTES

1. B.R. Ambedkar: 'The Buddha and His Dhamma', in *Dr Babasaheb Ambedkar Writings and Speeches*, vol. 11, Bombay: Education Department, Government of Maharashtra, Introduction.
2. Kshatriya (means warrior) is the second class or caste in the *Chaturvarna.*
3. B.R. Ambedkar: 'The Buddha and His Dhamma', op. cit., p. 4.
4. Ibid., pp. 10–11.
5. Ibid., p. 12.
6. Ibid., p. 23.
7. Ibid., p. 25.
8. Ibid., pp. 25–6.
9. Ibid., p. 28.
10. Ibid., p. 35.
11. Ibid., p. 34.
12. Ibid., p. 56.
13. Ibid., pp. 57–8.

14. Ibid., pp. 61–2.
15. Ibid., pp. 63–9.
16. Ibid., p. 75.
17. Ibid., p. 77.
18. Ibid., pp. 82–8.
19. Ibid., p. 91.
20. Ibid., p. 92.
21. Ibid., pp. 113–14.
22. Ibid., p. 121.
23. Ibid., p. 122.
24. Ibid., pp. 122–8.
25. Ibid., p. 129.
26. Ibid., p. 135.
27. Ibid., p. 137.
28. Ibid., pp. 141, 179–87.
29. Ibid., pp. 144–9.
30. Ibid., p. 146.
31. Ibid., p. 148.
32. Ibid., pp. 167–8.
33. Ibid., p. 185.
34. Ibid., p. 186.
35. Ibid., pp. 187–8.
36. Ibid., p. 203.
37. Ibid., pp. 204–7.
38. Ibid., pp. 207-9.
39. Ibid., pp. 188–90.
40. Ibid., pp. 193–6.
41. Ibid., pp.196–200.
42. Ibid., pp. 199–200.
43. Ibid., p. 200.
44. Ibid., p. 459.
45. Ibid., pp. 464–5.
46. See for the details of rules for *upasakas*: ibid., pp. 459–67. Also for the details of rules for *Bikkhus*: ibid., pp. 415–21.
47. Ibid., pp. 417–18.
48. See for the detail instruction concerning the rules of Sangha: ibid., pp. 415–17.
49. Ibid., p. 583.
50. Ibid., p. 229.

51. Ibid., p. 232.
52. Ibid., p. 234.
53. Ibid., p. 337.
54. Ibid., p. 339.
55. Ibid., p. 241.
56. Ibid., p. 245.
57. See for detail discussion: ibid., pp. 249–78.
58. See for detail discussion: ibid., pp. 281–309.
59. Ibid., p. 279.
60. Ibid., p. 131.

CHAPTER 2

Dalits and the Conversion

The conversion of the dalits from Hinduism to other religions was one of the main agendas of Dr B.R. Ambedkar's life since he fully believed that this was the only way for their liberation. He reached this conclusion after struggling for more than two decades for the basic human rights of the Dalits within the Hindu-fold. It is true that on 13 October 1935 he declared in a conference held at Yevala in Nasik his definite intention of changing his religion in the presence of more than 10,000 Dalits but his struggle towards this end began much earlier. This is proved by one of his articles written for the special number of *Telugu Samachar* in November 1926. I will refer to this article in this chapter later on, but before that it will be appropriate to quote here, part of the declaration which he made during the above conference. Dr Ambedkar addressed the Dalits present in the conference in these words:

> Because we have misfortune of calling ourselves Hindus, we are treated like thus. If we were members of another Faith, none would dare to treat us so. Choose any religion which gives you equality of status and treatment. We shall repair our mistake now.

After truthfully advising the Dalits, he made his personal declaration in these words:

> I had the misfortune of being born with the stigma of an Untouchable. However, it is not my fault; but I will not die a Hindu, for this is in my power.[1]

Therefore in this chapter I will discuss Dr Ambedkar's views on the conversion of the Dalits based on the following four documents written by him between 1926 and 1956, either in the form of articles or addresses for different occasions. These documents are:

i. 'Caste and Conversion' (originally published in the *Telugu Samachar* special number, November 1926.)[2]
ii. 'Why Conversion?' (originally given as address in Marathi at a Mahar Conference held on 30 and 31 May 1936 in Bombay).[3]
iii. 'Away from the Hindus' (written as reply to objections raised by the opponents against the declaration and resolution passed at the Mahar Conference of 30 and 31 May 1936).[4]
iv. 'The Great Conversion' (the speech delivered at Nagpur after the Great Conversion on 15 October 1956).[5]

The four major issues discussed in this chapter are:

i. Caste and conversion
ii. Why conversion?
iii. Main objections against the conversion of the Dalits
iv. The great conversion

Caste and Conversion

According to Dr Ambedkar, caste system has closed all the doors of Hinduism to conversion. But at the same time Hindu-Muslim riots of 1926 and the conversion movement carried on vigorously by the Muslims, became a matter of concern for the Hindu community. The notion prevailing among the Hindus that there is 'some native strength and stamina in its culture and civilization to make it survive' was shaken because they were being beaten by the Muslims both in physical as well as cultural struggle.[6] Dr Ambedkar also added another factor which made conversion of a large number of Hindus to Islam possible. He pointed out:

Fortunately for the Muslims there is a large mass of non-descript population numbering about seven crores which is classed as Hindus but which has no particular affinity to the Hindu faith and whose position is made so intolerable by that faith that they can be easily induced to embrace Islam. Some of these are going over to Islam and yet more may go.[7]

Among these 7 crores more than 4 crores were Dalits. Dr Ambedkar believed that this large number of Dalits and others, who were prone to conversion into Islam was a sufficient reason to cause alarm among the elite Hindus. He further said, 'If with a superiority of numbers the Hindus are unable to face the Muslims what would be their fate if their following was depleted by conversion to Islam? The Hindus feel that they must save their people from being lost to them and their culture.' According to Dr Ambedkar the answer to this question was found in the ritual of *Shuddhikaran* (reconversion), 'Herein lies the origin of the *Shuddhi Movement* or the movement to reclaim people to the Hindu faith.'[8]

Dr Ambedkar approached the problem of caste and conversion from other angle also. He asked is Hinduism a missionary religion? He referred to the answer given to this question by a number of scholars. For example Max Müller in his address given on 3 December 1873 in Westminster Abbey asserted that the Hindu religion was a non-missionary religion. Therefore based upon this belief some orthodox Hindus opposed the *Shuddhi* Movement. But then others supported it by referring to the stand taken by Jolly and Sir Alfred Lyall that in the ancient time Hinduism was a missionary religion and during that period Hindu rulers and priests spread this religion among the indigenous people of India and through conversion made them Hindu.[9] Dr Ambedkar added therefore that Hinduism was once a missionary religion, but for some reason it ceased to be that in course of its history.

Dr Ambedkar also discussed in detail the answer to the question, 'Why did the Hindu religion cease to be a missionary religion?' According to him the answer to this question has 'to be found in the fact that it developed the caste system'. 'The Hindu Society being a federation of castes and each caste being self-enclosed there is no place for the convert for no caste will admit him.' Here Dr Ambedkar referred to Aristotle, who once said that man (or woman) is a social animal. This means for an individual it is not possible to separate from his or her people. The social bond 'is established and rooted in the very growth of self-conscious'. Therefore life 'in real sense without society is no more possible for him or her than it is for a fish out of water'.

On the basis of the above argument, Dr Ambedkar stated, 'that before a society can make converts, it must see to it that its constitution provides for aliens being made its members and allowed to participate in its social life'. Otherwise 'If there is no such provision on conversion of an alien the question would at once arise where to place the convert. If there is no place for the convert there can be no invitation for conversion nor can there be an acceptance of it.' He said, 'the Hindu society is characterized by the existence of castes. Each caste is endogamous and lives by membership and does not allow any one from outside being brought into it'. Therefore Dr Ambedkar concluded, 'Caste is incompatible with conversion.' Therefore as long as caste system or even the feeling of the caste is there, conversion or reconversion (*Shuddhikaran*) has no meaning.[10]

WHY CONVERSION?

The conversion of the Dalits did not end in 1926 with the explanation given by Dr Ambedkar. To overcome this difficulty, the *Shuddhikaran*, the movement to reclaim people was started by some elite Hindus, but according to Dr Ambedkar it failed in strengthening the Hindu community. Within the next ten years, Dr Ambedkar reached a conclusion that 'change of religion' was the only way left for the Dalits. This was clear from his declaration at Yevala Conference on 13 October 1935, where he declared his intention that he 'will not die a Hindu'. Even at this conference, a resolution was passed:

> Now the Oppressed Classes must not spend money and manpower fruitlessly and must stop the fight on Satyagraha front. They must now consider their society separate from the Hindu society and organised the former to obtain for it an independent and respectable place in the country. Henceforth, all Depressed Classes must not take part in any Hindu religious festivals, Ratha, worships and other similar occasions.[11]

To assess the impact of the resolution and his declaration on the Mahar masses, on 30-1 May 1933 a Mahar Conference was convened, in which again publicly through a written address in Marathi, he explained to the masses 'Why Conversion?' or 'Why should the Dalits change their religion?'

According to Dr Ambedkar, any conversion had two important aspects–social and religious or moral and spiritual. But he also added, whatever may be the aspect or thinking about the 'conversion', it is important to understand the nature of untouchability. The problem of untouchability is a class struggle between Hindus and Dalits. In the case of Dalits, their struggles began as soon as they started claiming equal treatment. This struggle is permanent and has no end. It is as a struggle between slaves and masters. Dr Ambedkar sums up his argument about this struggle in these words:

> To put it straight, it can be said that the struggle between Hindus and the Untouchables is a permanent phenomenon. It is eternal, because of the religion which has placed you at the lowest level of the society is itself eternal, according to times and circumstances, is possible. You are at the lowest rung of the ladder today. You shall remain lowest forever. This means the struggle between Hindus and Untouchables shall continue forever.[12]

But will the Dalits survive this long struggle? This was the major question with which Dr Ambedkar was faced with, because to survive in such a struggle one needs 'strength'. There are three types of strengths, which include (1) manpower, since they are in a minority and are too unorganized (2) finance, which they hardly have because of no trades, no business, no service or land. The condition is still more bad, because mentally they have accepted their present state of life as part of the natural order. Their basic livelihood is the piece of left-over bread thrown by the so-called higher castes (3) mental strength, which according to Dr Ambedkar, Dalits do not have. Dr Ambedkar gave the example of Muslims, the secret of their survival was their strength and solidarity as a community. But according to him as long as they were a part of the Hindu community, they cannot except any support from within, it has to come from outside, which they can receive by associating with others through 'conversion'. He said to the dalits:

> From this you realise one thing, that unless you establish close relations with some other society, unless you join some other religion, you cannot get the strength from outside. It clearly means, you must leave your present religion and assimilate yourselves with some other society.[13]

The other important aspect of conversion was related to the spiritual well-being of a person. According to Dr Ambedkar, religion is, 'which governs people', but when this definition is applied to Hindu religion based society, one finds there is no place for an individual. 'The Hindu religion is constituted on a class-concept. Hindu religion does not teach how an individual should behave with another individual. A religion which does not recognize the individual is not personally acceptable to me.' In this regard he raised a question by saying, 'Three factors are required for the uplift of an individual. They are Sympathy, Equality and Liberty. Can you say by experience that any of these factors exist for you in Hinduism?'[14]

Dr Ambedkar even argued that the Dalits were not Hindus. He told the Dalits present in the conference, 'You are as separate from the Hindus as Muslims and Christians are.' Some people raised the question that if the Dalits get converted, the Hindu society will get divided. But he asserted further, 'By conversion, nobody can say or feel that one society has been split up. You will remain as separate from the Hindu as you are today, nothing new will happen on account of this conversion.'

Dr Ambedkar made it very clear that the aim of the Dalits was to gain freedom and 'this freedom cannot be secured without conversion'. Further conversion meant a total 'change of religion followed by the change of name will be more beneficial to you. To call oneself a Muslim, a Christian, a Buddhist or a Sikh is not merely a change of religion but also a change of name.'

Dr Ambedkar's above argument also referred to the history of conversion movement in India. Through the historical references, he actually dealt with the question of the ancestors' religion and their conversion. He said that the ancient Aryan religion was called Vedic religion and thousands of people followed it in India. But when Buddhism came, a large number of people left Hinduism and joined Buddhism. According to him this was because Hindu religion was not a religion but a slavery forced upon the people.

One of the main objectives of the Dalit movement was to achieve equality, which either could be achieved:

> by remaining in the Hindu-fold and another by leaving it by conversion. If equality is to be achieved by remaining in the Hindu-fold, mere removal of the sense being a touchable or an untouchable will not serve the purpose. Equality can be achieved only when inter-caste dinners and marriages take place. This means that the *chaturvarnya* must be abolished and the Brahmanic religion must be uprooted. Is it possible?. . . Of course not. The path of conversion is far more simpler than this. The Hindu society gives equality of treatment to Muslims and Christians. Obviously the social equality is easily achieved by conversion.[15]

Dr Ambedkar in his address on the question 'Why conversion?', also dealt with a number of other questions. He told his listeners that caste system was actually part and parcel of Hinduism. Thus destroying caste system meant destroying the Hindu religion. On the other hand Islam and Christianity do not sanctify caste, it in fact condemns it. Therefore destroying castes among Christians or Muslims will not mean destroying these religions. They will, in fact, support such a move. Dr Ambedkar also argued that economic or political rights of the dalits will not be affected by conversion. Dr Ambedkar even preferred in going to the 'social strength' as compared to these rights,[16] therefore he gave an open call to the Untouchables or Dalits by saying:

> To get human treatment, convert yourselves
> *Convert* for getting organised.
> *Convert* for becoming strong.
> *Convert* for securing equality.
> *Convert* for getting liberty.
> *Convert* so that your domestic life may be happy.[17]

Main Objections Against the Conversion of the Dalits

The impact of the Mahar Conference of May 1936, specially the Dr Ambedkar's address and its result was not limited only to the Dalits alone, because it had also shaken the foundation of the orthodox Hindu community. Because of this many warnings and threats were announced against the Dalits specially against the Dalit leaders, who were behind the conversion movement. Dr Ambedkar summarized all the objections raised by the opponents in different forms under the following four categories (what he called 'Four Principal Objections'):

1. What can the Untouchables gain by conversion? Conversion can make no change in their status.
2. All religions are true, all religions are good. To change religion is a futility.
3. The conversion of the Untouchables is political in nature.
4. The conversion is not genuine, as it is not based on faith.

Dr Ambedkar very systematically answered these four objections in the above mentioned order.

IS CONVERSION GENUINE?

Dr Ambedkar started his discussion on the conversion by quoting the first examples from the European conversion history to the Christianity. King Clovis was convinced by Bishop Remigins, he was baptised, but not alone, his 3,000 followers were also baptised. He also quoted the cases of German, Danish, Swedish and Russian, who were baptised in the same way. He concluded by asserting the genuineness of the conversion of the dalits in these words:

> History records cases where conversion has taken place as a result of compulsion or deceit. Today religion has become a piece of ancestral property. It passes from father to son so it does inheritance. What genuineness is this in such cases of conversion? The conversion of the Untouchables if it did take place then it would take after full deliberation of the value of religion and the virtue of the different religions. How can such a conversion be said to be not genuine conversion? On the other hand, it would be the first case in history of genuine conversion. It is therefore difficult to understand why the genuineness of the conversion of the Untouchables should be doubted by anybody.[18]

IS CONVERSION POLITICAL IN NATURE?

What could be the political gain through their conversion? Also nobody ever has proved that there is any direct inducement to conversion of the Dalits. There may be an 'incidental advantage' in the form of political gain. But that cannot be considered a direct inducement. Dr Ambedkar made this point very clear, 'Unless therefore the opponents of the conversion prove that the conversion desired by the Untouchables is for political gains and for nothing else their accusation is baseless. If political gain is only an incidental gain then there is nothing criminal in conversion.' He also added that as far as the Dalits were concerned, they were already enjoying the political rights similar to the Muslims and the Christians. So if they get converted, it was not going to bring to them any new political rights. Therefore he added, 'Political gain has no connection with conversion. The charge is a wild charge made without understanding.'[19]

ARE ALL RELIGIONS SAME?

Here he began his discussion by agreeing with the fact that all religions hold a common view 'that the meaning of life is to be found in the pursuit of "good"'. But Dr Ambedkar also added that all the religions do not give a similar definition of 'good', because 'One religion holds that brotherhood is good, another caste and untouchability is good.'[20]

Besides having a different view about 'good' among the religions, Dr Ambedkar said, 'there are permanent differences in the method of promoting good as they conceive it. Are there not religions which advocate violence? Given these facts how can it be said that all religions are the same and there is no reason to prefer one to the other.'[21]

Dr Ambedkar continued his argument by pointing that all the religions are not same, as claimed specially by the Hindus who opposed the conversion. He pointed out that these opponents agreed with the science of comparative religion, which rejected the claims of all revealed religions that they are true and those which are not revealed are false.

> That revelation was too arbitrary, too capricious test to be accepted for distinguishing a true religion from a false was undoubtedly a great service which the science of comparative religion has rendered to the cause of religion. But it must be said to the discredit of that science that it has created the general impression that all religions are good and there is no use and purpose in discriminating them.[22]

IS THERE ANY GAIN BY CONVERSION?

The first three objections Dr Ambedkar agreed to were not very serious in nature. But the question 'What can Untouchables gain by conversion? Also, the view that 'conversion can make no change in the status of the Untouchables', needs a serious consideration. Therefore he dealt with it in detail.[23]

Dr Ambedkar began his reply to the above objection by stating that this objection was based on the assumption that religion was a purely personal matter between humans and God and it has nothing to do with social life. He disagreed with this view and suggested that the best way to deal with this question was to separate religion from theology. He pointed that basically religion is made of 'the usages, practices and observances, rites and rituals'. Theology according to him was secondary and its object was merely to rationalize the content of the religion. He gave the example of primitive times when religion was a body of fixed traditional practices, not a system of belief with practical applications. At that time Dr Ambedkar made it very clear that the primary content of religion was social, because:

> The Savage society was concerned with life and preservation of life and it is these life processes which constitute the substance and source of the religion of the Savage society. So great was the concern of the Savage society for life and the preservation of life that it made them the basis of its religion . . . what is true of the religion of the savage is true of all religions wherever things are found for the simple reason that constitutes the essence of religion. It is true that in the present day society with its theological refinement this essence of religion has become hidden from view and is even forgotten.[24]

Dr Ambedkar as mentioned above, said that the basic or primary things as part of religion include various practices, rites, rituals, etc. In his further discussion he pointed out more clearly that all these were actually related to 'the elemental facts of human existence such as life, death, birth, marriage etc. magic, taboo and totem are not the ends. They are only means. The end is life and the preservation of life.'[25] It is through these means an individual participates in the society. Therefore Dr Ambedkar concluded this part of his discussion by saying: 'The correct view is that religion like language is social for the reason that either is essential for social life and the individual has to have it because without it he cannot participate in the life of the society.'[26]

The next related point was the purpose and function of religion. He said that religion 'emphasizes, universalizes social values and brings them to the mind of the individual who is required to recognize them in all his acts in order to that he may function as an approved member of the society. But the purpose of religion is more than this. It spiritualizes them.'[27] Here another point is needed to be noted that these moral and social values, with which religion deals, can be called as 'spiritual', but are still connected with personal and social life.

> The foregoing discussion, although it was undertaken to show that religion is a social fact, that religion has a specific social purpose and a definite social function it was intended to prove that it was only proper that a person if he was required to accept a religion should have the right to ask how well it has served the purposes which belong to religion.[28]

Basing upon his above conclusion about the purpose and function of religion, Dr Ambedkar suggested to the Dalits that they need to ask the following questions about Hinduism as a religion–Does Hinduism recognize their worth as human beings? Stand for their equality? Extend to them the benefit of liberty? Help them to forge the bond of fraternity between them and the Hindus? Teach them that the Untouchables are their brothers? Say that it is a sin to treat the Untouchables as being neither man nor beast? Tell them to be righteous to the Untouchables? Preach to the Hindus to be just and humane? Inculcate the virtue of being friendly to them? Tell the Hindus to love the Untouchables, to respect them and to do them no wrong? Does Hinduism universalize the value of life without distinction?[29]

Dr Ambedkar's answer to all these questions was 'no', therefore he concluded, 'In Hinduism there is no hope for the Untouchables. But this is not the only reason why the Untouchables wish to quit Hinduism. There is another reason, which makes it imperative for them to quit Hinduism. Untouchability is a part of Hinduism.'[30]

The next question related to the same objection was whether the dalits will gain materially by changing their religion? Dr Ambedkar's answer was threefold. He confessed that there will be no economic gain, but then as Hindu they are also poor so they have nothing to lose. Politically the Dalits by changing their religion will also not lose any rights, because the community (Christian or Muslim) which they will join will also have these rights.[31] Socially the Dalits will gain immensely because by conversion they will be members of a community whose religion has universalized and equalized all values of life. Such a blessing is unthinkable for them while they are in the Hindu-fold.[32]

The other concern Dr Ambedkar discussed in details was related to the 'social isolation' and 'inferiority complex' of the Dalits. Will conversion help to end these two problems? On the question of 'isolation', he said that through conversion by entering into a new 'kinship', this problem will be solved.

> Kinship makes the community take responsibility for vindicating the wrong done to a member. . . . It is Kinship which generates generosity and invokes its moral indignation which is necessary to redress a wrong. Kinship is the will to enlist the support of the Kindred community to meet the tyrannies and oppressions. . . .

Specifically regarding the Dalits he added:

> For the Untouchables to establish their Kinship with another community is merely another name for ending their present state of isolation. Their isolation will never end so long as they remain Hindus. As Hindus, their isolation hits them from front as well as from behind. Notwithstanding their being Hindus, they are isolated from the Muslims and the Christians because as Hindus they are

aliens to all–Hindus as well as Non-Hindus. This isolation can end only in one way and in no other way. That way is for the Untouchables to join some non-Hindu community and thereby become its kith and kin.[33]

What are the consequences of isolation? These consequences according to Dr Ambedkar are: 'social segregation, social humiliation, social discrimination and social injustice . . . denial of justice, denial of opportunity . . . want of sympathy, want of fellowship and want of consideration . . . positive hatred and antipathy from the Hindus.' But he adds: 'By having kinship with other community on the other hand, the Untouchables will have within that communities equal position, equal protection and equal justice, will be able to draw upon its sympathy, its goodwill.'[34]

The next related question to kinship was: 'Why is conversion necessary to establish kinship?' Dr Ambedkar in his answer to this question went through the history of the development of the concept of kinship. According to this in the early stage common bloodline used to be the basis of kinship, but later 'common religion' also became the basis of kinship. Dr Ambedkar in support of his argument quoted the case of Naomi and Ruth from the Bible, according to which Ruth, a Mobite by race became the part of Naomi's Jew community by accepting latter's religion. Because the Naomi asked Ruth to leave her after the death of her husband (who was a son of Naomi), she replied, 'Thy people shall be my people, and thy God my God.'[35]

On the question of 'inferiority complex', Dr Ambedkar told, 'The inferiority complex of the Untouchables is the result of their isolation, discrimination and the unfriendliness of the social environment. It is these which have created a feeling of helplessness which are responsible for the inferiority complex which cost him the power of self-assertion.'[36] But once a Dalit comes out of isolation through conversion, this complex problem automatically dies.

The last question with which Dr Ambedkar dealt was, if the

conversion raised the general social status of the Dalits. His answer was 'yes'. In his explanation he stressed on the change of name, which according to him was very important, because 'Names are symbols. Each name represents association of certain ideas and notions about a certain object.' He gave a direct example of one of the Dalits' name, 'Untouchable', which he said 'is a bad name. It repels, forbids and stinks. The social attitude of the Hindu towards the Untouchable is determined by the very name "Untouchable". . . . People have no mind to go into the individual merits of each Untouchable, no matter how meritorious he is. All Untouchables realise this.' Therefore he adds further,

> There is a general attempt to call themselves by some name other than the 'Untouchables'. The Chamar call themselves Ravidas or Jatavas. The Doms call themselves Shilpakars. The Pariahs call themselves Adi-Dravidas, the Madigar call themselves Arundhatyas, the Mahars call themselves Chokhamela or Somavamshi and the Bhangis call themselves Balmiki's. All of them if away from their localities would call themselves Christians.[37]

Dr Ambedkar ended the long discussion by giving them a call for conversion by saying:

> The force of the argument, of course, rests on a view of religion which is somewhat different from the ordinary view according to which religion is concerned with man's relation to God and all that it means. According to this view, religion exists not for the saving of souls, but for the preservation of society and the welfare of the individual. It is only those who accept the former view of religion that find it difficult to understand how conversion can solve the problem of Untouchability.[38]

The Great Conversion

Finally, the conversion movement reached its climax on 14 October 1956, when he took the *Deeksha* (Initiation) into Buddhism. Dr Ambedkar himself summed up the story of his conversion and its impact upon him in his address delivered a day later on 15 October 1956 at Nagpur. He said:

I started the movement of renouncing the Hindu Religion in 1935 at Nasik and since then I have been continuing the struggle. A mammoth meeting was held at Yevala, in 1935 in which through a resolution a decision was taken to the effect that we should renounce the Hindu religion. In that meeting I had said that though born a Hindu because I could not help it, I would not die as a Hindu. This conversion has given me enormous satisfaction and pleasure unimaginable. I feel as if I have been liberated from hell.[39]

In the same address he also told, why he chose to embrace Buddhism. He said:

In fact this is not something new nor have we imported it from outside. Buddhism is the religion of this country. It is more than two thousand years old. I feel sorry for the fact that I did not embrace this religion earlier. The teachings of the Buddha are eternal but even then Buddha did not proclaim them to be infallible. The religion of Buddha has the capacity to change according to times a quality which no other religion can claim to have.[40]

In this address Dr Ambedkar also clarified a number of points which were raised by his opponents. For example, why he chose Nagpur for his conversion? His answer was because Nagpur is an important city historically for the Buddhists. The ancient tribals of Nagpur were non-Aryans and were oppressed by the Aryans, but they were saved by Lord Buddha from decay and extinction. The name of Nagpur was taken from the name of river 'Nag', because the Nagas were living at the banks of this river.[41]

Some people also raised a point about the economical and political losses of the Dalits, who followed Dr Ambedkar. About 2,50,000 people embraced Buddhism on 14 October 1956.[42] But Dr Ambedkar explained that it was not true and he told very emphatically to these people who raised this point in order to cause doubts in the minds of the Dalits: 'Self-respect is more important than the material gains. Our struggle is for honour, for self-respect, not only for the economic progress alone.'[43]

Dr Ambedkar gave many arguments in favour of their embracing the Buddhism. He argued even having 'education' did not help them to get rid of the cause of untouchability. He said, 'Unfortunately, Hinduism, which is founded on the ideologies of inequality and injustice leaves no room for the development of enthusiasm. So long as the Untouchables continue to slave under the yoke of Hinduism, a diabolical creed–they can have no hope, no inspiration, no enthusiasm for better life.'[44]

On the other hand Dr Ambedkar told his followers:

> If we have any hope it is by renouncing the Hinduism and following the path of the Buddha. Let us now consider the principles of Buddhism. The fundamental principle of Buddhism is equality. Of all the Bhikkhus who joined the Order in the time of the Lord Buddha about 75 per cent of the Bhikkhus belonged to the Brahmins caste and the remaining 25 per cent were the Shudras. Even then Buddhism was called the religion of the Shudras.[45]

At this point Dr Ambedkar referred to a parallel case of Christianity, when it made its way into Europe. Dr Ambedkar wrote at that time:

> When Christianity made its way into Europe, the situation in and around Rome was appaling. People did not get enough food to fill their bellies. They lived in abject poverty. But do you know who were the people who extended a sympathetic response to the call of Christianity when it penetrated into Rome. Not those who were convinced of its spirituality, but those miserable poor and oppressed people for whom porridge, distributed free of cost served as a meal. People who worked as slave and serfs for their Roman masters. The poor and the oppressed became converts to Christianity.[46]

Dr Ambedkar also added to this truth a judgement passed by Mr. Gibben, the renowned historian and author of the *Rise and Fall of the Roman Empire*, who very scornfully branded 'Christianity as a religion of the poor and the beggars. . . . Some people, here in India, will no doubt say that this Buddhism is the religion of the untouchables.'[47]

Dr Ambedkar in his address also dealt with reason why Buddhism did not spread in India. He said that this was because there was no systematic preaching of Dhamma and in order to fill this gap he asked his followers to take *Deeksha* and propagate Dhamma, because you have 'the right to convert others' to your faith. Therefore Dr Ambedkar exhorted his followers 'Go forth to liberate people'.[48]

NOTES

1. Quoted in: Eleanor Zelliot: *From Untouchable to Dalit*, New Delhi: Manohar, 1992, p. 206.
2. Dr B.R. Ambedkar: 'Caste and Conversion', in *Dr Babasaheb Ambedkar: Writings and Speeches*, vol. 5, complied by Vasant Moon, Bombay: Education Department, Government of Maharashtra, 1989, pp. 422–5.
3. Dr B.R. Ambedkar: 'Why Conversion'?, in *B.R. Ambedkar: Political Thinkers of Modern India*, edited by Verinder Grover, New Delhi: 1993, pp. 3–13.
4. Dr B.R. Ambedkar: 'Away from the Hindus', in *Dr Babasaheb Ambedkar, Writings and Speeches*, vol. 5, compiled by Vasant Moon, op. cit., pp. 403–21.
5. Dr B.R. Ambedkar: 'The Great Conversion', op. cit., pp. 74–91.
6. Dr B.R. Ambedkar: 'Caste and Conversion', op. cit., p. 422.
7. Ibid., pp. 622–3.
8. Dr B.R. Ambedkar: 'Dr Ambedkar at the Round Table Conference', in *Dr Babasaheb Ambedkar: Writings and Speeches*, vol. 2, compiled and edited by Vasant Moon, Education Department, Government of Maharashtra, Bombay, 1982, p. 503.
9. Dr B.R. Ambedkar: 'Caste and Conversion', op. cit., p. 423.
10. See for detail discussion: ibid., p. 424.
11. Quoted in: Rev. Dr K. David Pandyan: *Dr B.R. Ambedkar and the Dynamics of Neo-Buddhism*, New Delhi, 1996, p. 80.
12. Dr B.R. Ambedkar: 'Why Conversion?', op. cit., p. 4.

13. Ibid., p. 6.
14. Ibid., p. 7.
15. Ibid., pp. 8–9.
16. Ibid., p. 12.
17. Ibid., p. 13.
18. Ibid., pp. 404–5.
19. See for a detail discussion: ibid., p. 405.
20. Ibid., p. 405 (bottom).
21. Ibid., p. 406.
22. Ibid., p. 406 (bottom).
23. See for a detail discussion: ibid., pp. 406–21.
24. Ibid., p. 407.
25. Ibid., p. 408.
26. Ibid., p. 409.
27. Ibid., p. 409 (bottom).
28. Ibid., p. 411.
29. Ibid., pp. 411–12.
30. Ibid., p. 412.
31. At the time of British rule in India, the Muslims and Christians had political rights as 'religious minorities'.
32. Dr B.R. Ambedkar: 'Away from the Hindus', op. cit., p. 413.
33. Ibid., p. 415.
34. Ibid., p. 415–16.
35. Ibid., p. 417.
36. Ibid., p. 418.
37. Ibid., p. 419.
38. Ibid., pp. 420–1.
39. Dr B.R. Ambedkar: 'The Great Conversion', op. cit., p. 79.
40. Ibid., pp. 86–7.
41. Ibid., p. 75.
42. K. David Pandyan: op, cit., p. 103.
43. Dr B.R. Ambedkar: 'The Great Conversion', op. cit., p. 77.
44. Ibid., p. 81.
45. Ibid., p. 84.
46. Ibid., pp. 85–6.
47. Ibid., p. 86
48. Ibid., p. 91.

CHAPTER 3

Christianity and Dalit Christians

Christianity: A Possible Means of Bringing Social Justice

Dr B.R. Ambedkar probably was the first person who though not a Christian, yet looked at Christianity and its message seriously. This was the reason he used in his writings both directly and indirectly, the illustrations from the Bible to clarify a number of his beliefs. Along with Christianity, he also used other egalitarian religions. In one of his essays, 'A Warning to the Untouchables', he told the Dalits in very clear terms that they should not 'expect the Hindu religion to perform the mission of bringing about social justice. Such a task may be performed by Islam, Christianity, or Buddhism. The Hindu religion is itself the embodiment of inequality and injustice to the Untouchables. For it, to preach the gospel of justice is to go against its own being.'[1] Dr Ambedkar in order to explain the meaning of fraternity, gave a direct quotation from the Bible (Galatians 3: 28) and from the writings of a Christian Order, Pilgrim Fathers as follows:

> Fraternity is the name for the disposition of an individual to treat men as the object of reverence and love and the desire to be in unity with his fellow beings. This statement is well expressed by Paul when he said, 'of one blood are all nations of men. There is neither Jew nor Greek, neither bond nor free, neither male nor female; for yet are all one in Christ Jesus.' Equally well was it expressed when the Pilgrim Fathers on their landing and Plymouth said: 'We are knit together as a body in the most sacred covenant of the Lord . . . by virtue of which we hold ourselves tied to all care of each others' good and of the whole.' These sentiments are of the essence of fraternity.[2]

Again, how important is an 'individual' and one's moral responsibility? This aspect of life is important, because it gives a due place to an 'individual as centre of social purpose'. To make his this point clear he quoted a passage from the Book of Prophet Ezekiel (18: 4, 20) of the Old Testament in which God recognizes the worth of an individual person in these words:

Behold! All souls are mine; as the soul of the Father, so also the soul of the son is mine; the soul that sinneth it shall die . . . the son shall not bear the inequity of the Father, neither shall the father bear the inequity of the son; the righteousness of the righteous shall be upon him, and the wickedness of the wicked upon him.[3]

Dr Ambedkar also compared the stories of creation of man in the Bible and the *Rigveda* and raised an important question of concerning the explanation of the origin of the four social classes. He wrote:

No theology has made it its purpose to explain the origin of classes in society. Chapter I of the Genesis in the Old Testament, which can be said to be analogous in intention and purpose to the *Purusha Sukta*, does nothing more than explain how man was created. It is not that social classes did not exist in the old Jewish society. Social classes existed in all societies. The Indo Aryans were no exception. Nevertheless, no theology has even thought it necessary to explain how classes arise. Why then did *Purusha Sukta* make the explanation of the origin of the social classes its primary concern?[4]

Dr Ambedkar in his other essay explained that higher classes would never accept Christianity because it meant surrendering their power and prestige drawn from the system of *Chaturvarna*. In this regard he said:

Applying this analysis of the working of the human mind it is clear that the Brahmin and the higher classes could never be receptive to the Christian doctrine. It preaches brotherhood of man and when applied leads to equality of man. Now the interests of the Brahmin and the higher classes is to maintain the system of *Chaturvarna*–

which is a system based upon inequality and which in the scale gave them a higher rank, greater opportunity to dominate and exploit the others. How can they be expected to accept Christianity? It means a surrender of their power and prestige.[5]

Christianity in India

In his essay 'Christianising the Untouchables', Dr Ambedkar made a very comprehensive analysis of the Christianity in India and its followers right from the beginning from the first century AD till 1931. According to 1931 census, the total population of India was 35,28,18,557 out of which 62,96,763 were Christians. Per cent wise it was 1.7 per cent. Dr Ambedkar raised a concern with this percentage because the growth of Christianity, according to Dr Ambedkar was very slow growth indeed. The question which he raised was, what are the causes of this slow growth. He gave three reasons. But before giving these he also narrated in brief a history of the Christian mission in India.

Dr Ambedkar traced back the history of Christianity to the second century. He also recognized the traditional view that Christianity came to India during the first century with the coming of St. Thomas, who was one of the twelve disciples of Jesus Christ, but there is no credible historical evidence available. Therefore he began the Indian Christian history with the coming of a first missionary namely Pantoenus, a Greek convert to Christianity.

In India, the real Christian missionary began with the coming of Vasco-de-Gama in 1497. But the most serious and determined missionary work began in 1542 with the coming of Francis Xavier, who carried on his activities with the support of Portuguese, and a large number of natives became members of the Roman Catholic Church.

The Protestants belonging to Lutheran Church traditions began their missionary work in 1706 at Tranquebar in south India. Their work was sponsored by the king of Denmark.

Among the well-known Protestant missionaries, Schwartz worked in Trichinopoly and Tanjore. In the north India, the first missionary group came to Calcutta in 1793 under the leadership of William Cary. In the end came the Anglican Church in 1813. But what were the causes of this poor result of the Christian missionary work in India? Dr Ambedkar in answer to this question has given following reasons:

i. The bad morals of the early European settlers in India
ii. The struggle between the Catholic and non-Catholic
iii. The wrong approach of the Christian missionaries

THE BAD MORALS OF THE EARLY EUROPEAN SETTLERS IN INDIA

Dr Ambedkar while referring to one of the earliest works of John William Kaye, *Christianity in India: An Historical Narrative* (1859), pointed out that there were some honest, decent men from the middle classes, who were sent to India, but large numbers were those who proved 'a disgrace' at home (in England). But those 'who had disgraced themselves at home would lead more respectable lives abroad'. To make his point further clear, Dr Ambedkar quoted number of cases of the early Europeans. For example, he quoted from Kaye's work about the first English settlers; about whom he says:

> There were, in truth, no outward motives to preserve morality of conduct, or even decency of demeanour, so from the moment of their landing upon the shores of India, the first settlers caste off all these bonds which had restrained them in their native villages, they regarded themselves as privileged beings–privileged to violate all the obligations of religion and morality and to outrage all the decencies of life. . . . They cheated, they gambled; they drank; they revelled in all kinds of debauchery. Associates in vice, linked together by a common bond of rapacity, they still often pursued one another with desperate malice, and, few though they were in numbers, among them there was no fellowship, except a fellowship of crime.[7]

The problem of bad morals among the early English settlers in India was not limited to the lower or middle level officers of the East India Company, it was spread among the high officials also. Kaye's two illustrations quoted by Dr Ambedkar proves this point:

The Deputy-Governor of Bombay was in 1669 charged as under: that he hath on the Sabbath day hindered the performance of public duty to God Almighty at the accustomary hour, continuing in drinking of health; detaining others with him against their wills; and whilst he drank, in false devotions upon knees, a health devoted to the Union, in the time appointed for the service belonging to the Lord's day, the unhappy sequel showed it to be but the projection of a further disunion. That to the great scandal of the inhabitants of the island, of all the neighbours round about, both popists and others that are idolators, in dishonour of the sobriety of the Protestant religion. . . .[8]

The above described bad moral condition not only prevailed during seventeenth century only, but also continued during eighteenth century. Dr Ambedkar quoted number of examples of eighteenth century, from which below is given of a well-known case of Lord Warren Hastings:

. . . those who ought to have set good example, did grievous wrong to Christianity by the lawlessness of their lives. . . . Hastings took another man's wife with his consent; Francis did the same without it. . . . It was scarcely to be expected that, with such examples before them, the less prominent members of society would be conspicuous for morality and decorum. In truth, it must be acknowledged that the Christianity of the English in India was, at this time, in a sadly depressed state. Men drank hard and gamed high, concubinage with the women of the country was the rule rather than the exception.[9]

Dr Ambedkar also added:

Such was the disorderliness and immorality among Englishmen in India. No wonder that the Indians marvelled whether the British acknowledged any God and believed in any system of morality. When asked what he thought of Christianity and Christians an Indian is reported to have said in his broken English–'Christian religion, devil religion; Christian much drunk; Christian much do wrong; much beat, much abuse others'–and who can say that this judgement was contrary to facts?[10]

THE STRUGGLE BETWEEN THE CATHOLIC AND NON-CATHOLIC

As seen earlier, the Roman Catholic missionary work began in India with the coming of Francis Xavier in 1541. But before the Roman Catholic Church, there already existed a Syrian Church in south India. Syrian Christians were mainly living on the coast of Malabar. They considered St. Thomas as their founding father and Syria as their spiritual home. The Patriarch of Babylon was their spiritual head. They did not know anything about the Pope or Church in Rome. But sadly, when the Portuguese, who represented the Roman Catholic Church, came to India, they started scandalizing the Syrian Christians and refused to accept them as Christians. Such views give birth to a conflict between the two Christian traditions.

The Goa based Catholic Church conducted an inquiry against the Syrian Christians, after which they started exerting pressure upon the Syrian Church to accept the supremacy of the Pope. The Bishop of the Syrian Church had to face the fury of Roman Catholic Church and at one stage they even lost the Bishop, who 'died after much trial and tribulation in his diocese'.[11] After this the Syrian Churches were only headed by an Archdeacon.

Meanwhile Rome appointed a very strong Archbishop at Goa namely Don Alex's de Menezes who increased the persecution upon the Syrian Christians. He even used the military power.[12] But the members of the Syrian Church refused to accept the supremacy of the Rome and rejected the wretched compromise agreed to by their Archdeacon.

But Menezes continued to suppress the Syrian Church. When he saw his direct attack has failed he tried other methods. 'Fraud took the place of violence, money took the place of arms. He bribed to those whom he could not bully and appealed to the imaginations of men when he could not work upon their fears. And little by little, he succeeded.' Finally the Archdeacon submitted to the Archbishop of Goa, who called a Synod meeting of the Syrian Church on 20 June 1599 at Diamper, in which he officially forced the Syrian Christians to accept 'yoke of Rome' after condemning the Patriarch of Babylon. The severe and grievous persecution started by Archbishop Menezes for a time is known as 'sixty years of servitude and hypocrisy', but during the later years though the faith of the Syrian Christians with the hard work of their missionaries was restored, yet the seeds of the conflict sown by Archbishop Menezes continued even afterwards.

There was no such open conflict between the Catholic Church and the Protestant Missionaries. There was however sufficient rivalry between them to prevent cooperation and conceited activity the lack of which also prevented a rapid growth of Christianity.[12]

THE WRONG APPROACH OF THE CHRISTIAN MISSIONARIES

The early missionaries assumed that their task of converting the masses would be easy if they succeeded in converting the Brahmins and higher classes of Hindu. They believed that the Brahmins held sway over the masses. The missionaries used two methods to do this. First, they started inviting public disputations with the learned Brahmins on the comparative merits of Christianity and Hinduism. They thought that the easiest way of converting the Brahmins was to defeat them in disputation and show them that their religion was wrong.[13] But according to Dr Ambedkar the missionaries could never win over the Brahmins by using this method.

There would be no common ground for the disputation between Hinduism and Christianity and where there is a common ground the Hindu could always beat the Christian. That there could be no common ground for disputation between Hindus and Christians is due to the fact that the two have a totally different attitude to the relations of theology to philosophy.[14]

Dr Ambedkar expanded the above point by adding:

Thus the Hindu speaks in terms of philosophy and the Christian speaks in terms of theology. There is thus no common ground for evaluation, or commendation or condemnation. In so far as both have theology–the Christians with their God and Jesus as his son and the Hindu with their God and his Avatars, the superiority of one over the other, depends upon the miracles performed by them. In this the Hindu theology can beat the Christian theology is obvious enough and just as absence of philosophy in Christianity is responsible for its failure to attract the Brahmin and the educated Hindu. Similarly the abundance of miracles in Hindu theology was enough to make Christian theology pale off in comparison.[15]

Dr Ambedkar concluded his discussion by saying: 'As events in India have shown this was a wrong approach. It was certainly just the opposite to the one adopted by Jesus and his disciples.'[16] Therefore, he added: 'This only shows that the people to whom Christianity made a natural appeal were the poorer classes and it is among them that Christianity first spread without the help of law or other extraneous advantage.'[17]

The other method, which the missionaries used was by opening schools, colleges, hospitals, etc. The use of this method also failed, because he says, 'The Brahmin and the higher classes have taken full advantage of the institutions maintained by the Christians Missions. But hardly any one of them has given any thought to the religion which brought these institutions into existence.'[18]

Dr Ambedkar offered his final argument by saying:

To have pursued them has been a vain effort and if the pursuit had been continued, I am sure there would have been no Christians in

India at all. The number of Christians we see in India today is due to the fact that some Christian Missionaries saw the futility of this. If they had not realized this error and started to win over the lower classes, there would have been no Christians in India at all. Even today hundreds and thousands of high caste Hindus take advantage of Christian schools, Christian colleges and Christian hospitals. How many of those who reap these benefits become Christians? Every one of them takes the benefit and runs away and does not even stop to consider what must be the merits of a religion, which renders so much service to humanity.[19]

Does the Indian Christian Community Count in India?

This is another important question which Dr B.R. Ambedkar not only raised, but also offered an answer. Part of his answer is in his discussion on the theme 'Gandhi and his opposition to Christianity'. Dr Ambedkar began this discussion by referring to the 'International Fellowship' which was held in 1928. In this fellowship representatives of different faiths met each other. Mahatma Gandhi was also present in this conference. According to Dr Ambedkar, it was Mahatma Gandhi who raised the issue of conversion in relation to the work of Christian missionaries. After this conference Mahatma Gandhi's opposition to the Christian missionaries' preaching and people getting converted to Christianity is well-known. He particularly objected to the spreading of the Christian Gospel among the untouchables. His antagonism to Christian missionaries and the conversion of untouchables to Christianity was based on certain propositions, which according to Dr Ambedkar were enunciated by him in quite unmistakable term. Dr Ambedkar selected four propositions to sum up Mahatma Gandhi's position:

i. My position is that all religions are fundamentally equal. We must have the same innate respect for all religions as we have for our own. Mind you, not mutual toleration but equal respect.

ii. All I want them (the Missionaries) to do is to live Christian lives, not to annotate them. Let your lives speak to us. The blind who do not see the rose, perceive its fragrance. That is the secret of the Gospel of the rose. But the Gospel that Jesus preached is more subtle and fragrant than the Gospel of the rose. If the rose needs no agents, much less does the Gospel of Christ need agents.

iii. The social work of the missions is undertaken not for its own sake, but as an aid to the salvation of those who receive social service. . . . While you give medical help, you expect the reward in the shape of your patients becoming Christians.

iv. I do maintain . . . that the vast masses of Harijans and for that matter, of Indian humanity, cannot understand the presentation of Christianity, and that, generally speaking, conversion, wherever it has taken place, has not been a spiritual act in any sense of the term. They are conversions of convenience. They (the Harijans) can no more distinguish between the relative merits (words omitted?) than can a cow. Harijans have no mind, no intelligence, no sense of difference between God and no-God.[20]

Dr Ambedkar raised another question concerning the position of Mahatma Gandhi. He has asked if Gandhi had shown a similar opposition to the conversion of the Untouchables to Islam.[22] His answer to this question was 'no'. But why? Dr Ambedkar quoted the view of a Christian, George Joseph, as answer to this question:

> The only difference is that there are 75 millions of Muslims and there are only 6 millions of Christians. It may be worthwhile making peace with Muslims because they can make themselves a thorn in the side of Nationalism: Christians do not count, because they are small in numbers.[22]

His final observations in this regard were:

> It is difficult to understand why Mr. Gandhi argues that services rendered by the missionaries are baits or temptations. Why is it not possible to believe that these services by missionaries indicate that service to suffering humanity is for Christian an essential requirement of their religion?. . . .

No body will deny to Mr. Gandhi the right to save the Untouchables for Hinduism. But in that case he should have frankly told Missions 'stop your work, we want now to save the Untouchables, and ourselves. Give us a chance!' It is pity that he should not have adopted this honest mode of dealing with the menace of the Missionaries. Whatever anybody may say I have no doubt, all the Untouchables, whether they are converts or not, will argue that Mr. Gandhi has been grossly unjust to Christian Missions. . . .

This attitude of Mr. Gandhi need not deter either the missionaries or the Untouchables. Christianity has come to stay in India and, unless the Hindu in their zeal for nationalism misuse their political, social and economic power to suppress it, will live and grow in numbers and influence for good.[23]

•

Dr Ambedkar finally agreed that one of the reasons why Indian Christian 'did not count' even in the writings of a person like Mahatma Gandhi, was the smallness of their number. But beside this general reason, the other obvious reasons for such a position of the Christians was:

i. One is this: the Indian Christians are living in sheltered waters. They are, at any rate, a large majority of them are living in the laps of the missionaries. For their education, for their medical care, for religious ministration and for most of their petty needs they do not look to Government. They look to the Missions. If they were dependent upon Government they would be required to mobilize, *to agitate, educate and organise* their masses for effective political action. For without such organisation no Government would care to attend to their needs and their requirements. . . .[24]
ii. The second reason is that the Indian Christian is a disjointed–it is a better word than the word disunited–community. All that it has in common is a common source of inspiration. Barring this one thing which they have in common everything else tends to keep them apart. Indian Christians like all other Indians are divided by race, by language and by caste. Their religion has not been a sufficiently strong unifying force as to make difference of language, race and caste as though they were mere distinctions. On the contrary their religion which is their only

> cement is infected with denominational differences. The result is that the Indian Christians are too disjointed to have a common aim, to have common mind and to put a common endeavour. . . . In short, the term Indian Christian is just a statistical phrase. There is no community feeling behind this phrase. Indian Christians are not bound together by what is consciousness of kind, which is the test of the existence of a community.[25]

Dalit Christians and their Conditions

Dr Ambedkar in his essay on 'The Condition of the Convert' raised a number of questions with regard to the condition of Untouchable converts to Christianity. Among these questions, three questions are basic: *One*, how much Christian missionaries have succeeded in meeting the basic needs of Untouchables? *Two*, has Christianity succeeded in raising the status of the Untouchables to the level of touchables? And *third*, has Christianity been able to save the Untouchable converts from the sufferings and the ignominy which is the misfortune of everyone who is born an Untouchable?

While dealing with the first question concerning the achievements of Christianity from the point of view of both Christian mission and of the Dalits, Dr Ambedkar accepted that in the field of social service they have done very good work. But he also asked: (a) Are these services the required needs of the Indian Christian community (b) Are there needs of the Indian Christian community which have not been attended to by the missionaries? Before answering these questions he suggested a criterion, which should be kept in mind while making any judgement on the social services of the missionaries. He said:

> It is necessary to bear in mind that Indian Christians are drawn chiefly from the Untouchables and, to a much less extent, from low ranking Shudra castes. The Social Services of Mission must therefore, he judged in the light of the needs of these classes. What are their needs?[26]

Dr Ambedkar also pointed out that the service rendered by the missionaries was mainly in the field of education and medical relief, which was beyond the ken of the Indian Christians specially the Dalit Christians. He further added these mostly go to the benefit of the high caste Hindus.

> The Indian Christians are either too poor or two devoid of ambition to undertake the pursuit of higher education. High schools, colleges and hostels maintained by the Missions are, therefore, so much misplaced and misapplied expenditure from point of view of the uplift of Indian Christians. In the same way much of the medical aid provided by the Missions goes to the Caste Hindus. . . . I have no doubt that this correctly sums up the position. If this is so then the money and energy spent by the Christian Missions on education and medical relief is misapplied and do not help the Indian Christians.[27]

Dr Ambedkar while continuing in the same breath his discussion on the needs of Indian Christians particularly the Dalit Christians, concluded with these words:

> The Indian Christians need two things. The first thing they want is the safeguarding of their civil liberties. The second thing they want is ways and means for their economic uplift. I cannot stop to discuss these needs in all their details. All I wish to point out is that this is a great desideratum in the social work the Christian Missions are doing in India.[28]

Dr Ambedkar after discussing the role of the social work offered by the Christian missionaries in the field of education and medical, dealt with the second question: Have the untouchable converts (Dalit Christians) risen to the status of touchable? or have the touchable and Untouchable converts discarded caste? In an answer to these questions, he gave a long quotation from the memorandum submitted by Dalit Christians of south India to the Simon Commission which throws a flood of light on the position of the Dalit Christians:

> We are by religion Christians, both Roman Catholics and Protestants. Of the total population of Indian Christians of the Presidency, the converts from the Depressed Classes form about sixty per cent. When the Christian religion was preached in our lands, we, the

Pallas, Pariahs, Malas, Madigas, etc., embraced Christianity. But others of our stock and origin were not converted and they are known to be the Hindu Depressed Classes, being all Hindus or adherents to the Hindus in religion. In spite, however, of our Christian religion which teaches us fundamental truths the equality of man and man before God, the necessity of charity and love for neighbours and mutual sympathy and forbearance, we, the large number of Depressed Class converts remain in the same social condition as the Hindu Depressed Classes. Through the operation of several factors, the more important of them being the strong caste retaining Hindu mentality of the converts to Christianity, and the indifference, powerlessness and apathy of the Missionaries, we remain today what we were before we became Christians–Untouchables–degraded by the laws of social position obtaining in the land, rejected by Caste Christians, despised by Caste Hindus and excluded by our own Hindu Depressed Class brethren.

The small proportion of the Christians of south India, whose representatives are found in the Legislative Council, say, in Madras, are caste Christians, a term which sounds a contradiction, but which, unfortunately, is the correct and accepted description of high caste converts from Hinduism, who retain all the rigour and exclusiveness of caste. Particularly in the Mofussil parts and the villages, they who ought to be our fellow Christians follow all the orthodox severity and unreason of caste exclusion; they damn us as 'Panchamas or Pariahs' and ignore our Christian claims and in the fulness of their affluence, power, prestige and position exclude us poorer Christians from society, . . . Frequent outburts of anti-Panchama activity are the scandal of the south Indian Christian life, and the least attempt on our part to better our lot, forward our progress and assert our elementary rights call down the wrath and fury of every man–official and non-official–Christian or Hindu, who claims a foolish superiority of birth. Denying the very foundations of Christianity, contrary to all love and charity and brotherhood, our 'fellow-Christians' treat us even in the Churches as Untouchables and Unapproachables, and relegate us to separate accommodation removed from their precincts and barricade their portions by means of iron rails and walls and fencings. There are several such churches.

In the matter of reception of sacraments, a most ridiculous segregation is practised to avoid pollution; our claims to educate our children and train them for life are ruthlessly denied and through sheer prejudice our children are denied access to schools, convents, hostels, boarding houses, or if admitted, are assigned an ignominous separate accommodation. Tracing his descent from high caste Hindu progenitors, the caste Christian looks for social status and position and finds favour in the eyes of his fellow caste-men, the Hindus. He treats the Depressed Class Christians in the same way as the Hindu Depressed Classes are treated by the Hindu caste people.[29]

In the above memorandum the expression used for the 'Dalit' is 'Depressed Class'. It reveals to us the following main points:

1. Though the Christian faith teaches the equality of all human beings, yet the Dalit converts to Christianity remained in the same social condition as the Hindu Dalits.
2. The small proportion of Christians, who represented in the Legislative Council were so called higher caste Christians.
3. In the matter of reception of sacraments in the Church, a most ridiculous segregation was practised to avoid pollution.
4. The education to the children of Dalit Christians were ruthlessly denied by denying to them the access to schools, hostels, boarding homes and convents.
5. The so called caste Christians treat the Dalit Christians in the same way as the Dalit Hindus were treated by the caste Hindus.

Dr Ambedkar also pointed out that Christianity failed to wipe out the pagan practices of the converts. They continued to follow the social and religious ritual and practices of the Hindus. All these were incompatible with the Christian faith and way of life. Why has Christianity not been able to stamp them out? To find the answer to this question, Dr Ambedkar studied in detail the Church history of the various missions in India and came to the following conclusion:

The answer is that the Christian Missionaries although they have been eager to convert person to Christianity have never put up a determined fight to uproot paganism from the Convert. Indeed they have tolerated it.[30]

Dr Ambedkar in support of his above conclusion quoted number of examples from the well known Missions by which he proved, how they openly tolerated pagan practices. For example an Italian Jesuit, Father Robert de Nobili, who came to India in 1608, even declared himself a 'Roman Brahmin' and became a *Sanyasi*. Through forgery he produced the 'Fifth Veda'. An Anglican missionary Rev. Robert Noble, who came to India in 1841 and worked in Masulipattam while defending the caste in the Church, gave the following argument:

> The humblest and most pious Christian present in England would not allow their sons, much less their daughters, to be educated with their footmen, with their cooks and scullery maids. . . . My Father would not have allowed us to mix with the cook's or stable boy's children; nor can I see it right to require of Brahmins that before we will teach them the Gospel, they must sit down on the same form with the pariah and the sweeper. The requirement is to me unreasonable and unchristian.[31]

Dr Ambedkar closed his discussion on the root cause of the practice of caste in the Church by saying:

> In adopting this policy the missionaries never thought that some day, somebody would ask them, 'What good is Christ-ianity for a Hindu if it does not do away with his caste.' They misunderstand their mission and thought that making a person Christian was the same thing as making him a follower of Christ.[32]

The next question, which Dr Ambedkar dealt with was: Has Christianity been able to save the convert from the suffering and the ignominy which is the misfortune of every one who is born an untouchable? The answer is 'no'. But what are the reasons for this failure? According to Dr Ambedkar, a change in the social status of the convert could have been the result of a twofold change. First, there must be a change in the attitude of the Hindus (or even caste Christians). Secondly, there must be a change in the mentality of the converts (Dalit Christians). This twofold change can only take place if both the groups move from their old positions. In the case of caste Hindus or caste Christians, nothing has been done, so no change has taken place in the basic attitude.

With regards to the other part of the above question: Does Christianity inspire the Untouchables to move on? Again the answer is 'no'. Because according to Dr Ambedkar:

> Christian preaching to the Untouchable is less centered on 'practical' reforms and more centered around the development of Christian social attitude. Christians who desires the conversion of the Untouchables insists on regarding Christianity as purely 'spiritual'. To teach that Christianity have obligation to love other is no doubt very valuable. But to stop there and argue that spiritual life expressed in a social attitude is quite unrelated to material life and Christians can have nothing to do with it, is in my judgement to preach an empty doctrine. . . . The Christian Missionaries have never thought that it was their duty to *act* and get the injustice that pursues the Untouchables even after his conversion to Christianity removed. That Missions should be so inactive in the matter of the social emancipation of the Untouchable is of course a very sad thing. But far more painful is the inaction of the Untouchable who becomes a convert to Christianity. . . I have never noticed the Untouchable Christians meeting in Conferences for the redress of their social wrongs. . . . Why is it then there has been no movement for the redress of their wrongs?[33]

Dr Ambedkar further gave three reasons for the failure of Dalit Christians to raise a movement:

1. The first reason is the complete absence of desire among the educated Christians (both non-dalits and dalits) to take up the cause of the community and fight it. Because there is no community feeling among the educated class and the mass. They are divided into high class and low class without having any concern for one another. The result is that Dalit Christians are leaderless and therefore unable to mobilize for the redress of their wrongs.
2. The second reason is to be found in the mental make-up of the Dalit Christians, which is 'characterized by a complete absence of any urge to break his bonds' with the past or with their

old faith. A Dalit might become a Christian. 'But the case is very rare of an untouchable becoming a Christian because of a positive discontent or dislike of the Hindu religious teachings. The result is that Christianity becomes only an addendum to his old faith.'

3. The third reason for the absence of any urge is due to the teachings of the Christian Church. The teaching that the fall of humanity is due to his/her sin and the reason why one must become Christian is because in Christianity there is promise of forgiveness of sins.

Dr Ambedkar adds:

Whatever may be the theological and evangelistic basis of these doctrine there is no doubt with disaster. This Christian teaching is a direct challenge to sociology which holds that the 'fall of man is due to an unpropitious environment and not to the sins of man'. Here the problem is not whether the sociological view is right or wrong, but that the above doctrine misleads the humanity and sets them on a wrong trail. This is what exactly happened with the Dalit Christians. Instead of being taught that their fall was due to a wrong social and religious environment and that for their improvement they must attack the environment, they were taught their fall was due to their sin. Consequently the Dalit Christians instead of being empowered to conquer their environmental context, conferred themselves with the belief that there is no use struggling, for the simple reason that their fall is due to the sin committed not by them but by some remote ancestors of their called Adam and Eve. Here Dr Ambedkar stressed a point that when a Dalit Christian 'was a Hindu his fall was due to his *Karma*. When he becomes a Christian he learns that his fall is due to the sins of his ancestor. In either case there is no escape for him.'[34]

Epilogue

Now the question which arises is why he showed keen interest by going to the depth of Dalit Christians problem and pointed out the serious weakness of Christian missionary work or Christianity in India. Dr Ambedkar answered this question in these words:

I do not know what Indian Christians will think of what I have said of the weaknesses which infect their life. One thing I can say. It is this–I am deeply interested in Indian Christians because a large majority of them are drawn from the Untouchable classes. My comments are those of a friend. They are not strictures of an adversary. I have drawn attention to their weaknesses, because I want them to be strong, and I want them to be strong because I see great dangers for them ahead. They have to reckon with the scarcely veiled hostility of Mr. Gandhi to Christianity taking its roots in the Indian social structure. But they have also to reckon with militant Hinduism masquerading as Indian Nationalism. What this militant Hinduism will do to Christians and Christianity can be seen from what happened at Vrindavan very recently. If newspaper reports are true a crowd of mild Hindus quietly went and burned down the Mission buildings in Vrindavan and warned the missionary that if he rebuilt it they would come and burn it down again! This may be the solitary instance of misguided patriots or this may be just a piece of what the Hindus are planning to get rid of Christians and Christianity. If it is the shadow of events to come then Indian Christians must be prepared to meet them. How can they do that except by removing the weaknesses I have referred to? Let all Indian Christian ponder.[35]

NOTES

1. *Dr Babasaheb Ambedkar: Writings and Speeches*, vol. 5, Bombay: Education Department, Government of Maharashtra, 1989, p. 398.
2. *Dr Babasaheb Ambedkar: Writings and Speeches*, vol. 3, Bombay: Education Department, Government of Maharashtra, 1987, p. 97.
3. Ibid., p. 99.
4. *Dr Babasaheb Ambedkar: Writings and Speeches*, vol. 7, Bombay: Education Department, Government of Maharashtra, 1990, p. 28.
5. *Dr Babasaheb Ambedkar: Writings and Speeches*, vol. 5, op. cit., p. 444.
6. See for detail discussion: ibid., pp. 430–44.
7. Ibid., pp. 430–1.
8. Ibid., p. 431.

9. Ibid., pp. 432–3.
10. Ibid., p. 434.
11. Ibid., p. 435.
12. See for detail discussion: ibid., p. 437–8.
13. Ibid., p. 438 (bottom).
14. Ibid., p. 439.
15. Ibid., pp. 439–40.
16. Ibid., p. 441.
17. Ibid., p. 443.
18. Ibid., p. 439.
19. Ibid., p. 444 (bottom).
20. Ibid., p. 446.
21. Ibid., p. 447.
22. Ibid., p. 448.
23. Ibid., p. 450.
24. Ibid., p. 475.
25. Ibid., p. 476.
26. Ibid., p. 452.
27. Ibid., pp. 452–3.
28. Ibid., p. 453.
29. Ibid., pp. 454–5.
30. Ibid., p. 456.
31. Ibid., p. 469.
32. Ibid., p. 470.
33. Ibid., p. 471–2.
34. See for detail discussion: ibid., pp. 471–2.
35. Ibid., p. 476.

CHAPTER 4

Dalits: A Minority

Dr B.R. Ambedkar's views on 'Dalits: A Minority' are evident in a number of his writings. But I will limit my discussion mainly to the five documents, which are now available under the title *Dr Babasaheb Ambedkar: Writings and Speeches*, in volumes 1 and 2. These documents are: (1) Evidence before the Southborough Committee on Franchise (1919), (2) Evidence before the Indian Statutory Simon Commission (1928), (3) The Round Table Conferences (1930–1), (4) States and Minorities–What are Their Rights and How to Secure Them in the Constitution of Free India (1947), and (5) Thoughts on Linguistic States (1955). The whole discussion of this chapter is divided under the following three sub-heads:

i. Dalits' Own Identity
ii. Dalits: A Minority
iii. Protection and Safeguards for the Minorities

Dalits' Own Identity

Dr B.R. Ambedkar's goal in life was to protect the rights of the Dalits at all cost. He was also clear that their rights cannot be fully protected as long as are clubbed with a larger community of Hindus. For him as a community 'they are distinct and separate from the Hindus, a separate element in the national life of India'. Because Dalits are 'separate element', therefore according to Dr Ambedkar 'as a separate and distinct element it is entitled to constitutional safeguards'. He further added 'An element, making a claim for constitutional safeguards, must show that it is definable as separate and distinct from the rest. If it shows that it is separate and distinct, its right to constitutional safeguards is held admissible.'[1] This was the basis according to Dr Ambedkar for the provisions concerning the safeguards of the rights of the various minority groups in the Constitution.[2] Dr Ambedkar offered a very systematic and comprehensive explanation in his 'The Real Issue–Aren't the Untouchables a Separate Element?'[3] In this essay one of the main arguments, he offered was:

> One more point must be stressed. On the foregoing analysis the Untouchables may be classed as a Hindu if the word Hindu is used in the religious but in the limited sense of a follower of a recognized cult. Even here, there is a necessity for giving a warning against concluding that the Hindu and the Untouchable have a common religion. The fact is that even as followers of recognized cults they cannot be said to have a common religion. The exact and appropriate expression would be to say they have a similar religion. A common religion means a common cycle of participation. Now, in the observances of the cults there is no such common cycle of participation. The Hindus and the Untouchables practise their cults in segregation so that notwithstanding the similarity of their cults they remain separate as two aliens do. . . . The only test which can be of use is its social sense as indicating a member of the Hindu society. Can an Untouchable be held to be part of the Hindu Society? Is there human tie that binds them to the rest of the Hindus? There is none. . . . There is not even the right to touch, much less to associate. . . . The whole tradition of the Hindus is to recognise the Untouchable as a separate element and insist upon it as a fact. The traditional terminology of the Hindus to distinguish Hindus and Untouchables. According to this traditional terminology, the Hindus are called *Savarnas* and the Untouchables are called *Avarnas*. It speaks of the Hindus as *Chaturvarnikes* and the Untouchables as *Panchamas*.[4]

It is clear from Dr Ambedkar's above arguments that for him, Dalits had their own 'independent identity' even as part of the Hindu religion. His struggles to establish this identity of the Dalits continue throughout his life. Because of this independent identity, the Dalits, he believed are to be considered as one of the minorities. He also cleared this position while giving evidence on behalf of the Dalits before the Southborough Committee in 1919. His position further becomes clear from the arguments which he offered during the Round Table Conferences in 1930–1 and the position taken in the memorandum submitted to the Constituent Assembly on behalf of the All India Scheduled Caste Federation in 1947 under the title 'States and Minorities–What are Their Rights and How to Secure Them in the Constitution of Free India'. Here briefly these three documents are examined in order to get the gist of views. But before going through these three documents, I will first briefly look into the concept of 'minority' as interpreted by Dr Ambedkar with special references to the Dalits or Untouchables.

Dalits: A Minority

Dr Ambedkar's view on the meaning of 'minority' and its application specially for the Dalits, is available in a number of his addresses and documents made and prepared by him. But his most clear statement on this issue is in his address, to the second sitting of the 'Sub-Committee No. III' on Minorities on 31 December 1930. The expression used at that time for the Dalits was the 'Depressed Classes', about whom Dr Ambedkar told the Committee. 'On the other hand, if you take the Depressed Classes, they are a minority, which comes next to the great Muslims minority in India, and yet their social standard is lower than the social standard of ordinary human beings.'[5] For Dr Ambedkar 'social standard' was/is one of the main factors to define a 'minority'. Generally both at the levels of international and national 'number' has been accepted criterion to define a minority,[6] but in the case of Dr Ambedkar, there are other factors which need to be taken into account while defining and also giving a weightage to their needs. His following observation makes this point very clear:

In our opinion weightage is to be conceded because a minority is weak, either in number, or because its social standing is low, or its educational standing is backward as compared with others, or because its economic strength is not sufficient to place it on a fighting power with other communities.[7]

Here in Dr Ambedkar's general observation it becomes very clear that while he recognized the principle of population ratio to define a minority, he also very strongly suggested that other factors included 'social standing', 'educational standing' and 'economic strength'. In the case of the Dalits as a distinct minority, Dr Ambedkar while giving his evidence before the Simon Commission on 23 October 1928, made his position very clear by saying:

The first thing I would like to submit is that we claim that we must be treated as a distinct minority, separate from the Hindu community. Our minority character has been hitherto concealed by our inclusion in the Hindu community, but as a matter of fact there is really no link between the Depressed Classes and the Hindu community. The first point, therefore, I would stress before the Conference is that we must be regarded as a distinct and independent minority, Secondly, I would like to submit that Depressed Classes minority needs far greater political protection than any other minority in British India, for the simple reason that it is educationally very backward, that it is economically poor, socially enslaved, and suffers from certain grave political disabilities, from which no other community suffers.[8]

Dr Ambedkar made the above points repeatedly clear. For example, one of the main political demands of Dr Ambedkar was to have a separate electorate for the Dalits and offered the following argument in defence of his demand:

To say that the Scheduled Castes are not a minority is to misunderstand the meaning of the word 'minority'. Separation in religion is not the only test of a minority. Nor is it a good and effective test.

Social discrimination constitutes the real test for determining whether a social group is or is not a minority. Even Mr. Gandhi thought it logical and practical to adopt this test in preference to that of religion separation. Following that test, Mr. Gandhi in an editorial under the heading 'The Fiction of Majority' in the *Harijan* dated 21 October 1939 has given his opinion that the Scheduled Castes are the only real minority in India.[9]

So from the above discussion drawn from the various documents prepared by Dr Ambedkar between the period 1928–47, it becomes very clear that Dalits are indeed a 'minority'.

Protection and Safeguards for the Minorities

Dalits are without any doubt a minority like Muslims or Christians but why do they need protection? Dr Ambedkar made this point very clear in his opening address of the second sitting of the Sub-Committee (Minorities) on 31 December 1930:

> On the other hand, if you take the Depressed Classes, they are a minority, which comes next to the great Muslim minority in India, and yet their social standard is lower than the social standard of ordinary human beings. Again, if you take the minorities and classify them on the basis of social and political rights, you will find that there are certain minorities which are in enjoyment of social and political rights, and the fact that they are in minority does not necessarily stand in the way of their full and free enjoyment of these civic rights. But if you take the case of the Depressed Classes, the position is totally different. They have in certain matters no rights, and where they have any, the majority community will not permit them to enjoy them.[10]

In this observation, Dr Ambedkar was very clear in presenting a case of the Depressed Classes as a minority and he in the same address, also suggested very clear-cut criteria for the protection of a minority. According to him it is necessary, 'because a minority is weak, either in numbers or because its social standing is low, or its educational standing is backward as compared with others, or because its economic strength is not sufficient to place it on a fighting par with other communities'.[11] The fear regarding the minorities was spelled out in the following words:

> Having said all that I need say let me add one thing in conclusion that this whole question of minority representation is really the crux of the whole situation, and if the majority community desires that all minorities should associate with them in having or in claiming constitution which will give India what they call Dominion Status, or what we prefer to call Government by the people for the people and in the name of the people, then I am afraid that the majority community must see to it that all fears of the minorities are set at rest. Otherwise it may be possible for us to take what I do not conceal from myself in the risk that most of us are taking in claiming Dominion Status.[12]

Dr Ambedkar in the seventh sitting of the Round Table Conference on 28 September 1931, in the meeting of the 'Minorities Committee' once again laid an emphasis that the Committee should equally take care of the needs of the weaker minorities such as 'the Depressed Classes, the Anglo-Indians and the Christians'[13] along with the Hindus, Muslims and Sikhs. He also made it clear that in the process of transfer of power, the care should be taken 'that the power shall be shared by all communities in their respective proportions'.[14]

Regarding the status and rights of the Depressed Classes or Untouchables Dr Ambedkar was clear that this in fact was for him a fundamental issue, in one of his addresses in 1945 by saying:

> It is wrong to say that the problem of the Untouchables is a social problem. For, it is quite unlike the problems of dowry, widow remarriage, age of consent, etc., which are illustrations of what are probably called social problems. Essentially, it is a problem of quite a different nature in as much as it is a problem of securing to a minority liberty and equality of opportunity at the hands of a hostile majority which believes in the denial of liberty and equal opportunity to the minority and conspires to enforce its policy on the minority.

Viewed in this light, the problem of the Untouchables is fundamentally a political problem.[15]

Dr Ambedkar's complete views about the 'minorities' is found in a document (brochure), which he submitted on 3 March 1947 to the Constituent Assembly on behalf of the All India Scheduled Castes Federation. This document was a memorandum on the safeguards for the Scheduled Castes, entitled 'States and Minorities–What are Their Rights and How to Secure Them in the Constitution of Free India'. The document actually contained in it a draft Constitution and it also presents the basic thoughts of Dr Ambedkar about the content of the Constitution. In this document he considered the Scheduled Castes even more than a minority. From his preface of this document, it appears that he came to the conclusion that his opponents were not going to accept the fact that Scheduled Castes were in real sense a minority. Therefore in this document, he proposed three sets of rights: 'the Rights of Citizens, of Minorities, and of the Scheduled Castes'.[16]

Besides confirming the rights of the minorities which are enjoyed by all other citizens, all the fundamental rights along with the remedies against invasion of these rights, he specially recommended four sets of protection of minorities, which included (a) protection against communal executive, (b) protection against social and official tyranny, (c) protection against social boycott, and (d) power of Government of India including purposes beneficial to the minorities.[17]

He also asked for proportional representation in the Legislative as well as in the Executive for the minorities based upon their (a) economic position, (b) social status, and (c) educational qualification.[18] Dr Ambedkar was totally against the British model of Parliamentary Executive, which did not have any place for the role of minorities. About this he said:

The British System of Government imposes no obligation upon the Majority Party to include in its cabinet the representation of Minority

Party. If applied to India the consequence will be obvious. It would make the majority community a governing class and the minority community a subject race. It would mean that a communal majority will be free to run the administration according to its own ideas of what is good for the minorities. Such a state of affairs could not be called democracy. It will have to be called imperialism.[19]

His main concern behind such an argument was that the Constitution of free India should evolve 'a mechanism to enable a minority to return its true representative to Legislative'.[20]

From the later writings of Dr Ambedkar namely 'Thoughts on Linguistic States' (1955) another point becomes very clear that his ideas were not only based upon some vague ideas, but on the actual ground reality (what he called 'Ground Plan'). From the 'Ground Plan' he meant 'the social structure of a community', to which according to him 'the political plan is sought to be applied' and 'in the case of India the social structure is built up on the caste system', the consequences of which 'on politics are quite obvious'.[21] The negative effects of this system upon the political rights of the minorities have been summarized by Dr Ambedkar in these words:

1. Voting is always communal. The voter votes for the candidate of his community and not for the best candidate.
2. The majority community carries the seat by sheer communal majority.
3. The minority community is forced to vote for the candidate of the majority community.
4. The votes of the minority community are not enough to enable the candidate to win the seat against the candidate put up by the majority community.
5. As a consequence of social system of graded inequality the votes of the higher (major) communities can never condescend to give his vote to a candidate of a minority community. On the other hand the voter of the minority community who is socially on a lower level takes pride in giving his vote to the candidate of the majority community. That is another reason why a candidate of a minority community loses in election.[22]

To deal with the above situation Dr Ambedkar suggested 'a mechanism', by which the minorities particularly the Dalits can represent in the government at different levels. In his evidence before the Southborough Committee (1919) in this regard he made the following suggestion:

> We, have, therefore two possible methods of meeting the situation: either to reserve seats in plural constituencies for those minorities that cannot otherwise secure personal representation, or grant communal electorate. Both have their usefulness.[23]

Why the above two methods 'reservation of seats' or 'communal electorates' should be granted to the Dalits as a minority? Interests will not be protected by being included in the majority community Hindu. In this case he argued that this was because even as part of the Hindu community they do not enjoy the basic human rights and their interests are not protected by the majority. He says:

> The Untouchables are usually regarded as objects of pity but they are ignored in any political scheme on the score that they have no interests to protect. And yet their interests are the greatest. Not that they have large property to protect from confiscation. But they have their very *persona* confiscated. The socio-religious disabilities have dehumanised the Untouchables and their interests at stake are therefore the interests of humanity. The interests of property are nothing before such primary interests.[24]

Dr Ambedkar in his evidence to the Southborough Committee told that:

> The Untouchable is not even a citizen. Citizenship is bundle of rights such as (1) personal liberty, (2) personal security, (3) rights to hold private property, (4) equality before law, (5) liberty of conscience, (6) freedom of opinion and speech, (7) right of assembly, (8) right of representation in a country's government, and (9) right to hold office under the State. . . . These are the interests of the Untouchables. And as can be easily seen they can be represented by Untouchables alone. They are distinctively their own interests and none else can

truly voice them. . . . Untouchability constitutes a definite set of interests which the Untouchables above can speak for. Hence it is evident that we must find the Untouchables to represent their grievances which are their interests and, secondly, we must find them in such numbers as well as constitute a force sufficient to clam redress.[25]

Dr Ambedkar's above-mentioned views show that from the beginning of his struggle, he wanted his community to represent a separate and distinct community like Muslims or Christians and enjoy the status of minorities, because that was the only way they could represent their interests themselves, which nobody else could do on their behalf.

Finally, what Dr Ambedkar stressed in his document on 'Status and Minorities' (1947) reveals why he wanted Dalits' right to be protected in the Constitution. In this document he said:

Unfortunately for the minorities in India, Indian Nationalism has developed a new doctrine which may be called the Divine Right of the Majority to rule the minorities according to the wishes of the majority. Any claim for sharing of power by the minority is called communalism while the monopolizing of the whole power by the majority is called Nationalism. Guided by such a political philosophy the majority is not prepared to allow the minorities to share political power nor is it willing to respect any convention made in that behalf . . . under these circumstances there is no way left but to have the right to the Scheduled castes embodied in the Constitution.[26]

From Dr Ambedkar's writings and his thoughts expressed in this chapter, it becomes very clear that the minorities in general and the Dalits as 'a minority' particularly for him were not only an issue, with which he dealt throughout his life, in fact the people belonging to various minorities and the protection of their rights were part of his life mission.

NOTES

1. Dr B.R. Ambedkar: 'The Real Issue–Aren't the Untouchables a Separate Element?', in *Dr Babasaheb Ambedkar: Writings and Speeches* edited by Vasant Moon, vol. 9, Bombay: Education Department, Government of Maharashtra, 1991, pp. 181–2.
2. Ibid., p. 182.
3. Ibid., p. 181–98.
4. Ibid., pp. 183–4.
5. Dr B.R. Ambedkar: 'The Round Table Conferences', in *Dr Babasaheb Ambedkar: Writings and Speeches*, edited by Vasant Moon, vol. 2, Bombay: Education Department, Government of Maharashtra, 1982, p. 529.
6. James Massey, *Minorities in a Democracy: The Indian Experience*, New Delhi, Manohar, 1999, pp. 25, 41.
7. Dr B.R. Ambedkar: 'The Round Table Conferences, op. cit., p. 533.
8. Ibid., p. 465.
9. Dr B.R. Ambedkar: 'Status and Minorities–What are Their Rights and How to Secure Them in the Constitution of Free India', in *Dr Babasaheb Ambedkar: Writings and Speeches*, complied by Vasant Moon, vol. 1, Education Department, Government of Maharashtra, Bombay, 1989, p. 422.
10. Dr B.R. Ambedkar: 'The Round Table Conference', op. cit., p. 529.
11. Ibid., p. 533.
12. Ibid., p. 534.
13. Ibid., p. 658.
14. Ibid., p. 662.
15. Dr B.R. Ambedkar: 'The Real Issue–Aren't the Untouchables a Separate Element?' op. cit., p. 190.
16. Dr B.R. Ambedkar: 'Status and Minorities–What are Their Rights and How to Secure Them in the Constitution of Free India' (1947), op. cit., p. 385.
17. Ibid., pp. 398–400.
18. Ibid., pp. 401–2.
19. Ibid., p. 413.
20. Ibid., p. 424.
21. Dr B.R. Ambedkar: 'Thoughts on Linguistic States' (1955), in

Dr Babasaheb Ambedkar: Writings and Speeches, vol. 1, Bombay: Education Department, Government of Maharashtra, 1979, p. 168.

22. Ibid., p. 168.
23. Dr B.R. Ambedkar: 'Evidence Before the Southborough Committee on Franchise' (1919), in *Dr Babasaheb Ambedkar: Writings and Speeches*, compiled by Vasant Moon, vol. 1, Bombay: Education Department, Government of Maharashtra, 1989, p. 252.
24. Ibid., p. 255.
25. Ibid., p. 256.
26. Dr B.R. Ambedkar: 'Status and Minorities–What are Their Rights and How to Secure Them in the Constitution of Free India' (1947), op. cit., pp. 427–8.

CHAPTER 5

Framing the Constitution

'Dr Ambedkar who as a man has been able to show to the world that the Scheduled Castes are no less important a man they can rise to heights and give to the world their great services. I know, Sir, that he has served the community of the Harijans and also of India by his great service and sacrifice in preparing a Constitution which will be the order of the day from 26 January 1950. . . .'[1] testified a fellow Dalit, V.I. Muniswamy Pillay of Madras on 17 November 1949, the day the third and the final reading of the Draft Constitution began. Beside Pillay, there were other members of the Constituent Assembly who recognized the great work and service of Dr B.R. Ambedkar in framing the Constitution of India. Seth Govind Das described him as 'the Manu of the present age'.[2] M. Ananthasayanam Ayyangar added that Dr Ambedkar came to doubt and to criticize but ultimately took the 'charge of this Constitution and framed it'.[3] S. Nagappa in his tribute said, 'Well sir, this has proved to what heights Dr Ambedkar, though he is a member of the Scheduled Classes, if an opportunity was given, can arise. He has proved this by his efficiency and ability in the way he has drafted and piloted this Constitution.'[4] A very interesting testimony came from Syamanandan Sahaya of Bihar who compared the achievement of Mahatma Gandhi and said: '. . . the achievement of independence would go to the credit of Mahatmaji, and its codification to one of Mahatmaji's worst critics, viz., the great architect of our great Constitution, Dr Ambedkar. Dr Ambedkar, Sir, deserves the gratitude not only of this

Assembly but of this Nation.'[5] R.V. Dhulekar of United Province offered a more personal tribute to Dr Ambedkar by saying, 'Dr Ambedkar has performed a very great work. I would not say Herculean because that is a very small word. He has performed a task worth of great Pandava Bhim and worthy of the name that he has–Bhim Rao Ambedkar–He has certainly justified his name–Bhim Rao–and he has performed the task with clarity of vision, clarity of thoughts and clarity of language.'[6] K.M. Jedhe of Bombay while joining with his earlier colleagues added that Dr Ambedkar 'has framed Bhim Smrithi'[7] in the form of the Indian Constitution.

The above are only some of the tributes paid by the members of the Constituent Assembly at the time of final reading of the Draft Constitution, which was the result of the hard work of Dr B.R. Ambedkar as the Chairman of the Drafting Committee and his colleagues. It took two years, eleven months and seventeen days from 9 December 1946 onwards. But if one carefully reads the Draft Constitution and the Dr Ambedkar's works (which appeared in different forms from 1919, when he gave evidences before the Southborough Committee and till his submission of a memorandum 'Status and Minorities–What are Their Rights and How to Secure Them in the Constitution of Free India' to the Constituent Assembly in 1946), one will find that Indian Constitution certainly is the work of Dr B.R. Ambedkar. The former President of India, His Excellency Dr K.R. Narayanan, in his foreword to the vol. 13 of *Dr Babasaheb Ambedkar: Writings and Speeches*, affirmed this by writing:

> As Chairman of the Drafting Committee and as the one who piloted this historic document through the Constituent Assembly, he was the principal architect of the Constitution.[8]

As mentioned above, the immediate story of the framing of Indian Constitution began with the first meeting of the Constituent Assembly and it closed on 26 January 1950, when the final draft of the Constitution was approved by the

Constituent Assembly and adopted by the people of India as its Constitution. What happened during almost three years period and how much Dr Ambedkar contributed in its framing, is put together in one volume of 1,240 pages in *Dr Babasaheb Ambedkar: Writings and Speeches*, vol. 13 under the title *Dr Ambedkar, the Principal Architect of the Constitution of India.* Here in the present work I am dedicating only this chapter in which I will limit my discussion mainly on the three most important addresses of Dr B.R. Ambedkar. These addresses are:

1. Address on the resolution moved in the Constitution Assembly by Pandit Jawaharlal Nehru regarding the aims and objectives of the proposed Constitution on 17 December 1946.
2. Address to the Constituent Assembly while moving the first draft of the Constitution on 4 November 1948.
3. Address on the completion of the Draft Constitution on 25 November 1949.

These three addresses also represent the three stages of the period, which the Constituent Assembly took in preparing the Constitution. The discussion here is based upon the above three addresses will be carried on under the following three sub-heads:

i. Aims and Objectives of the Constitution
ii. The Form of the Constitution
iii. Completion of the Constitution

Aims and Objectives of the Constitution

After the Second World War in 1945, the British government gave a serious thought to granting freedom to India. In fact in order to deal with the smooth transfer of power, it sent three persons' team to India, which was named Cabinet Mission with a proposal, in which suggestion was made to set up a Constituent Assembly to frame a Constitution for the future governance of India. The Constituent Assembly was to be composed of representatives chosen by the members of the Provincial Legislature Assemblies. But the Cabinet Mission divided the Provincial Legislatures into three categories: (1) Muslims, (2) Sikhs, and (3) General. Each of these categories was given a fixed quota of seats. It is interesting to note that the category 'general' included in it: (1) Hindus, (2) Scheduled Castes, (3) Indian Christians, and the Anglo-Indians. The scheduled castes once again were disturbed that instead of considering them a separate element, 'they were lumped together with the Hindus'.[9]

Because of the scheme for electing the members to the Constituent Assembly, Dr Ambedkar could not get elected from Bombay, because of the opposition of Congress. Therefore he tried and succeeded in becoming the member of the Constituent Assembly through the Bengal Assembly under 'general' category. The Constituent Assembly had its first meeting on 1 December 1946 which out of 296 members was attended by 207 members only. The Muslim League had boycotted the Constituent Assembly.[10] For the first meeting Dr Sachidanand Sinha, a senior most member was elected the Provisional Chairperson. Then on 11 December 1946, Dr Rajendra Prasad was elected the Permanent Chairperson of the Constituent Assembly.[11] Finally it was on the 13 December 1946, the work on the future Constitution began with a 'Resolution' containing the 'Aims and Objectives', moved by Pandit Jawaharlal Nehru. Pandit Nehru cleared in his introductory remarks the purpose of this resolution by saying: 'The Resolution that I am placing before you defines our aims, describes an outline of the plan and points the way which we are going to tread.'[12] The text of the proposed 'Resolution' is reproduced below:

1. This Constituent Assembly declares its firm and solemn resolve to proclaim India as an Independent Sovereign Republic and to draw up for her future governance a Constitution;
2. Wherein the territories that now comprise British India, the

territories that now form the Indian States, and such other parts of India as are outside British India and the States as well as such other territories as are willing to be constituted into the Independent Sovereign India, shall be a Union of them all;

3. Wherein the said territories, whether with their present boundaries or with such others as may be determined by the Constituent Assembly and thereafter according to the Law of the Constitution, shall possess and retain the status of autonomous Units, together with residuary powers, and exercise all powers and functions of government and administration, save and except such powers and functions as are vested in or assigned to the Union, or as are inherent or implied in the Union or resulting therefrom;
4. Wherein all power and authority of the Sovereign Independent India, its constituent parts and organs of government, are derived from the people;
5. Wherein shall be guaranteed and secured to all the people of India justice, social, economic and political; equality of status, of opportunity, and before the law; freedom of thought, expression, belief, faith, worship, vocation, association and action, subject to law and public morality;
6. Wherein adequate safeguards shall be provided for minorities, backward and tribal areas, and depressed and other backward classes;
7. Where in shall be maintained the integrity of the territory of the Republic and its sovereign rights on land, sea, and air according to justice and the law of civilised nations; and
8. This ancient land attains its rightful and honoured place in the world and make its full and willing contribution to the promotion of world peace and the welfare of mankind.[13]

The above 'Resolution' was discussed and debated in the Constituent Assembly before it was adopted. Number of questions and doubts were raised by the members. Serious questions related to the Muslim League members' participation was raised by leading members, which included Purushottam Das Tandon, M.R. Jayakar and Syama Prasad Mookerjee. P.D. Tandon raised question about the integrity of Muslim

League,[14] M.R. Jayakar spoke in favour of the participation of Muslim League and even moved an amendment to the Resolution,[15] which created a tense atmosphere in the Assembly. It is in this situation the President Dr Rajendra Prasad by passing over more than 20 other persons, invited Dr Ambedkar on 17 December 1946 to speak to the House on the 'Resolution' dealing with the 'Aims and Objectives'. Even Dr B.R. Ambedkar was surprised because he was expecting his turn on the next day. He accepted the invitation and stood to speak. By that time everybody knew Dr Ambedkar's feeling towards Congress. He was a known opponent of Congress and its ideology. Thus when Dr Ambedkar arose to speak, according to his biographer Dhananjay Keer:

> The House was all attention. Ambedkar took a view of the House. Everybody now thought that Ambedkar, by playing such a dangerous role, would go under with the mover of the amendment. To rise against the will and objectives of the Congress bosses, who were the nation's most powerful leaders, was to meet one's Waterloo! The Congress members were ready with their hands raised to smash their avowed enemy and throw him down.[16]

But it did not happen that way. The result of Dr Ambedkar's address was amazing, but positive. Dhananjay Keer summed up its importance very nicely, in these words:

> So forceful was the passionate appeal that it produced an excellent impression upon the Constituent Assembly. He was frequently cheered by the Congress members. Dr Jayakar speech containing the same appeal aroused resentment while Ambedkar's fine oration evoked a sense of co-operation in their minds, and the hands that were itching to smash him rang with approbation! It was red-letter day in the amazing life of Ambedkar. The sacrileger had become now a counsel, the scoffer had become a friend who cast a spell on the Congress men. Few speeches have given such a turn to the life of a speaker. The consideration of the resolution was postponed to another session, which was to meet in January, and it was passed on 28 January 1947.[17]

Here only we are highlighting the main points of that address.

RIGHTS WITHOUT REMEDIES ARE NO RIGHTS

Dr Ambedkar divided his address in two parts. In part one, he dealt with the clauses 5, 6 and 7 of the Resolution which set out the objectives of the future Constitution. These clauses spelled out the basic rights of people in general and weaker sections in particular. It also dealt with the sovereign rights of the country as a nation. This part Dr Ambedkar called 'non-controversial'. In the second part of his address he dealt with the clauses 1 to 4, to which he called 'controversial'. These clauses dealt with 'the future Constitution of India' specially with the powers of the Central and State governments.[18]

In the first part of the address, the main point made was that whatever is proposed in these clauses has been done under the influence of 'the Rights of Man', which were pronounced by the French Assembly about 500 years ago. These 'rights' or 'safeguards' look merely as a formality, because he said: 'The Resolution although it enunciates certain rights, does not speak of remedies. All of us are aware of the fact that rights are nothing unless remedies are provided whereby people can seek to obtain redress when rights are invaded.'[19] This was the reason Dr Ambedkar in the beginning of his address said: 'I must confess that, coming as the Resolution does from Pandit Jawaharlal Nehru who is reputed to be a socialist, this Resolution, although non-controversial is to my mind very disappointing.'[20]

Dr Ambedkar in his first part of the address made his above point further clear. He pointed out that even the usual formula that no person's 'life, liberty and property will be taken without the due process of law', had not been included in the Resolution. The Resolution made the proposed fundamental rights 'subject to law and public morality', but who will determine, what is 'law' or 'public morality'? It is 'left to the

Executive of the day'. Again the Resolution has suggested some provision concerning justice, economical, social and political rights, but in order to implement these rights Dr B.R. Ambedkar pointed out the Resolution should explicitly state that 'there would be nationalization of industry and nationalization of land. I do not understand how it could be possible for any future government which believes in doing justice socially, economically and politically unless its economy is a socialistic economy.'[21]

NEED FOR A STRONG CENTRE

The second part of the address was more difficult, because in it he dealt with the controversial part of the Resolution containing clauses 1 to 4. The controversy as Dr Ambedkar put 'centred on the use of word "Republic"'. In clause 4 the meaning of sovereignty was that it 'is derived from the people'. So if the real power of the government is vested in the people and their elected representatives, then according to Dr B.R. Ambedkar, Dr Jayakar's views were correct that without the Muslim League's representatives, it will not be proper to deal with the Resolution. Dr Ambedkar while accepting all kinds of divisions based upon castes and creeds still positively hoped that one day there would be a 'United India', which would include Muslims also. But that is in the future and according to him, 'our difficulty is not about the ultimate future. Our difficulty is how to make the heterogeneous mass that we have today taken a decision in common and march on the way which leads us to unity. Our difficulty is not with regard to the ultimate, our difficulty is with regard to the beginning.' It was to overcome this difficulty with the 'beginning' and to make a move towards 'unity', he made a sincere appeal by saying 'in order to induce every party, every section in this country to take on to the road it would be an act of greatest statesmanship for the majority party even to make a concession to the prejudices of people who are not prepared to march together and it is for that, that I propose to make this appeal'.[22]

Besides the above appeal Dr Ambedkar raised a number of other related questions and made some very important points, which later on became the basis for the future Constitution of India. From the contents of the Resolution particularly clauses 2 and 3, it become very clear that the mover of the Resolution had in mind the Cabinet Mission's proposals concerning the content of the Constitution. Dr Ambedkar specially raised a question with clause 3, which talked about the territorial units either which were parts of the British India or which were outside, when these units join the free India these will 'retain the status of autonomous units, together with residuary powers'. It is true that the Resolution talked about 'two different sets of polity', but it did not refer 'to the idea of a union of Provinces or grouping of Provinces'. Dr Ambedkar very strongly and clearly put forward the idea 'a strong united Centre'. In fact he added that he wanted a 'much stronger centre, than we had created under the Government of India Act of 1935'. Clause 3 of the Resolution was the main point of difference, which gave the reason to Muslim League to boycott the Assembly. It is also true that clause 3 fulfilled the requirements of the Cabinet Mission's proposals and legally the Assembly could adjust the Resolution without the presence of Muslim League. But Dr Ambedkar here again raised an important question related to 'power' and 'wisdom'. 'Power' or 'authority', which was rested in the Constituent Assembly allowed it legally to decide the thing, whatever way it thought the best. But the question Dr Ambedkar raised was 'whether it would be wise, whether it would be statesman like, whether it be prudent to do so at this stage'. He himself answered this question by saying:

> [I]t would not be prudent, it would not be wise. I suggest that another attempt may be made to bring about a solution of the dispute between the Congress and the Muslim League. This subject is so vital, so important that I am sure it could never be decided on the mere basis of dignity of one party or the dignity of another party. When deciding the destinies of nations, dignities of people,

dignities of leaders and dignities of parties ought to count for nothing. The destiny the country ought to count for everything.[23]

According to Dr Ambedkar, there were three ways to solve the problem related to Hindus and Muslims: (1) By surrendering of one party, (2) through negotiation, and (3) through open war. There were many members of the Assembly, who wanted to adopt the third way 'by the method of war', about which Dr Ambedkar said:

> If there is anybody who has in mind the project of solving the Hindu-Muslim problem by force, which is another name of solving it by war, in order to that the Muslims may be subjugated and made to surrender to the Constitution that might be prepared without their consent, this would be involved in perpetually conquering them. The conquest would not be once and forever I do not wish to take more time than I have taken and I will conclude by again referring to Burke. Burke has said somehow that it is easy to give power, it is difficult to give wisdom. Let us prove by our conduct that if this Assembly has arrogated to itself sovereign powers it is prepared to exercise then with wisdom. That is the only way by what we can carry with us all sections of the country. There is no other way that can lead us to unity. Let us have no doubts on that point.[24]

The result of Dr Ambedkar's views and appeal on the Resolution was that the discussion was postponed till the next session on 18 December 1946. Finally the Resolution was adopted on 21 December 1946.

THE FORM OF THE CONSTITUTION

After the adoption of the Resolution on 21 December 1946, the further work on the Constitution began on 24 January 1947. According to the Proposal of the Cabinet Mission an Advisory Committee on fundamental rights, minorities, etc., was constituted under the Chairmanship of Sardar Patel. The Committee had 50 members and Dr Ambedkar was one of them. To carry on the work more effectively, the Advisory Committee appointed the following four sub-committees:

1. Fundamental Rights Sub-committee
2. Minorities Sub-committee
3. North-East Frontier Tribal Areas Sub-committee
4. Excluded and Particularly Excluded Areas (other than those in Assam) Sub-committee

Dr Ambedkar was a member of the first two sub-committees and was fully involved. He also submitted a memorandum defining Fundamental rights, minority rights and safeguards for the scheduled castes to the fundamental rights sub-committees. This memorandum was later published in 1947 under the title 'States and Minorities–What are Their Rights and How to Secure Them in the Constitution of India'. This memorandum carried in it his ideas about the content of the Constitution.

The Constituent Assembly through a resolution on 30 April 1947 also appointed the following three other committees:

1. The Union Power Committee
2. The Union Constitution Committee
3. The Provisional Constitution Committee

Dr Ambedkar was a member of the Union Constitution Committee. His contribution was taken very seriously by everyone. One positive result of this was that when on the partition of Bengal, he ceased to be member of the Constituent Assembly, the Congress happily sponsored his candidature from Bombay for the membership of the Constituent Assembly. In fact Dr Rajendra Prasad, President of the Constituent Assembly himself through a letter requested to B.G. Kher, then Prime Minister of Bombay to elect Dr Ambedkar immediately. Dr Rajendra Prasad wrote in his letter, 'Apart from any other consideration we have found Dr Ambedkar's work both in the Constituent Assembly and the various committees to which he was appointed to be of such an order as to require that we should not be deprived of his services.'[25] So Dr B.R. Ambedkar was re-elected in July from Bombay as a member of the Constituent Assembly.

Later on the Drafting Committee was appointed, which had its first meeting on 30 August 1947 and elected Dr Ambedkar as its Chairman unanimously. The Committee sat from 27 October 1947 regularly for 44 days till 13 February 1948 and read, discussed and revised each article prepared by the office of the Constitutional Adviser. Dr Ambedkar himself conducted all the business of the Committee. The draft of the Constitution as settled by the Drafting Committee was submitted to the President of the Assembly on 21 February 1948. The Draft Constitution was made public continuously for eight months, in which suggestions and criticism were received. During this period also the Committee continued to function and considered the suggestions for amendment from time to time. Finally the Draft Constitution was presented to the Constituent Assembly on 4 November 1948 for the first meeting.[26] But before the reading took place, Dr Ambedkar introduced the Draft. In his introductory address, besides dealing with the two basic questions relating to the form of Government and the form of the Constitution, he also drew the attention of the House to some of the special features of the Constitution. Therefore I will draw attention to these areas under the following sub-heads:

(a) The form of Government
(b) The form of the Constitution
(c) Special features of the Constitution

THE FORM OF GOVERNMENT

The first point which Dr Ambedkar made clear was about the choice of a form of the Government, which the Draft Constitution proposed. There are two main forms of Governments— based upon the Parliamentary system and the Presidential system. The Draft Constitution opted for the first, the Parliamentary system. Dr Ambedkar gave a reason for this choice by referring to the Presidential System of America. The two systems he said are 'fundamentally different'.

Both the systems have President. But the President of America is the Chief Head of the Executive and the administration is directly under him. But on the other hand under the Draft Constitution, the President was the head of the State, but not of the Executive. He represented the nation, but did not rule the nation. Again the American President has under him Secretaries of different departments appointed by him and he has the power to remove them any time. But on the other hand, the President of the Indian Union, though has the Council of Ministers, but he does not have power to remove them as long as they enjoy a majority in the Parliament. The other difference of two systems is that under the American Presidential system, the Secretaries will not be members of the Congress, but in the Parliamentary system, the Ministers have to be the members of the Parliament.

The other difference is that the American system has only periodic assessment (once in two years), on the other hand Parliamentary system has both the daily as well as periodic assessments. In the case of India, the daily 'assessment is done by members of Parliament, through questions, Resolutions, No-confidence motions, Adjournment motions and Debates on Addresses. Periodic assessment is done by the Electorate at the time of the election which may take place every five years or earlier. . . . The Draft Constitution in recommending the Parliamentary system of Executive has preferred more responsibility to more stability.'[27]

THE FORM OF THE CONSTITUTION

Dr Ambedkar began this part of his address by stating that there are two known forms of the Constitution namely the unitary and the federal. Two important characteristics of the Unitary Constitution are: (1) the supremacy of the central polity, and (2) the absence of subsidiary of sovereign politics. On the other hand according to a Federal Constitution, (1) there will be a central and subsidiary politics side by side, and (2) each being sovereign in the field assigned to it. In other words, federation means the establishment of a dual polity. 'The Draft Constitution is, Federal Constitution in as much as it establishes what may be called a Dual Polity. This Dual Polity under the proposed constitution will consist of the Union at the Centre and the States at the periphery each endowed with sovereign powers to be exercised in the field assigned to them respectively by the Constitution.'[28]

Dr Ambedkar to make the above point clear again, referred to the American Constitution, which also follows a dual polity, but it differs fundamentally from the Indian dual polity. American dual polity offered a dual citizenship, under which each state can offer certain exclusive rights to its state citizens, but on the other hand Indian dual polity according to which all the Indian citizens have same rights of citizens, no matter in what state they reside. The other major point on which Indian Federal Constitution differ from the American Constitution is that no Indian state can form its own separate constitution, whereas American states can have their own constitution.

After stating the differences between the Indian Draft Constitution and the American Constitution, Dr Ambedkar also introduced some of the special features of the Draft Constitution, which are being discussed in the next sub-section.

SPECIAL FEATURES OF THE CONSTITUTION

It is true that the Constitution of the Union of India follows the federal system as described above. But at the same time it is also a unitary Constitution. So the first unique feature of Indian Constitution about which Dr Ambedkar said 'the Draft Constitution can be both unitary as well as federal according to the requirements of time and circumstances. In normal times, it is framed to work as a federal system. But in times of war it is designed as to make it work as though it was unitary system.'[29] How can this change take place? It was to be through a proclamation issued by the president, who was authorized under the Provision of Article 275. By using power given in this Article, once the president issues such a Proclamation, the Union can claim if it wants '(1) the power to legislate upon any subject even though it may be in the State list, (2) the power to give directions to the States as to how they should exercise their executive authority in matters which are within their charge, (3) the power to vest authority for any purpose in any officer, and (4) the power to suspend the financial provision of the Constitution.'[30]

The other special features of the Draft Constitution described by Dr Ambedkar was the way it dealt with the two basic weaknesses, 'rigidity' and 'legalism'. The Draft Constitution to deal with both of these weaknesses, provided two methods in the Constitution. First, it gave the Parliament power to legislate (under Article 226) when a subject became a matter of national concern as distinguished from purely Provincial concern, though the subject may be in the State list. The second method adopted to deal with above mentioned weakness was the provision for facility with which the Constitution could be amended.[31]

Another special feature of the Draft Constitution, was the way it distributed powers between the Union and States in legislative, executive and judiciary. But the Draft Constitution also provided means, which helped the Union to have uniformity in all the basic matters in order to maintain the unity of the country. These means adopted in the Draft Constitution were: (1) a single judiciary, (2) uniformity in the fundamental laws, civil and criminal, and (3) a common All-India Civil Service to man important posts.[32]

Dr Ambedkar while explaining the problem of majority and minority and how the Draft Constitution proposes to deal with it, said:

In this country both the minorities and the majorities have followed a wrong path. It is wrong for the majority to deny the existence of minorities. It is equally wrong for the minorities to perpetuate themselves. A solution must be found which will serve a double purpose. It must recognize the existence that it will enable majorities and minorities to merge someday into one. The solution proposed by the Constituent Assembly is to be welcomed because it is a solution which serves this two-fold purpose.

While referring to the Irish majority-minority problem in which one minority leader (Carson) told to the majority 'Damn your safeguards, we don't want to be ruled by you'. Dr Ambedkar said:

No minority in India has taken this stand. They have loyally accepted the rule of the majority which is basically a communal majority and not a political majority. It is for the majority to realize its duty not to discriminate against minorities. Whether the minorities will continue or will vanish mostly depends upon this habit of the majority. The moment the majority loses the habit of discriminating against the minority, the minorities can have no ground to exist. They will vanish.[33]

Another special feature of the Draft Constitution was the way it offered the Fundamental Rights. According to the criticism in the Draft Constitution, these are not absolute, whereas the Fundamental Rights should be absolute. But Dr Ambedkar gave the example of American Fundamental Rights which are also not absolute. He also referred to the differences between the 'non-fundamental rights' and 'fundamental rights', about which he said: 'the real distinction between the two is that non-fundamental rights are created by agreement between parties while fundamental rights are the gift of the law'. But he also added, 'Because fundamental rights are the gift of the State it does not follow that the State cannot qualify them.'[34] He also stated the reason, why the fundamental rights are not kept fully absolute in the Draft Constitution. He said:

What the Draft Constitution has done is that instead of formulating fundamental rights in term and depending upon our Supreme Court to come to the rescue of Parliament by inventing the doctrine of police power, it permits the State directly to impose limitations upon the fundamental rights. There is really no difference in the result. What one does directly the other does indirectly. In both cases, the fundamental rights are not absolute.[35]

Next to the Fundamental Rights came in the Draft Constitution the 'Directive Principles', which according to Dr B.R. Ambedkar was 'a novel feature in a Constitution framed for Parliamentary Democracy'. But the criticism about these Directive Principles was that they 'have no legal force behind them . . . they are useless because they have no binding force in law'. But Dr Ambedkar in his reply to this criticism said that he agreed with the first part of the criticism, but not the second part that 'they have no sort of binding force at all'. In his reply he further said:

> The Directive Principles are like the Instrument of Instructions, which were issued to the Governor-General and to the Governors . . . by the British Government under the 1935 Act. . . . What are called Directive Principles a merely another name for Instrument of Instructions. The only difference is that they are instructions to the Legislature and the Executive. Such a thing is to my mind to be welcomed. Wherever there is a grant of power in general terms for peace, order and good government, it is necessary that it should be accompanied by instructions regulating its exercise.

The other reason to include the Directive Principles in the Draft Constitution was to provide 'a machinery for the government of the government'. Dr Ambedkar further said that it may be true that no political party or groups in power 'have to answer for their breach in a court of Law'. But he added 'they certainly have to answer for them before the electorate at election time. What great value these directive principles will be realized better when the forces of right contrive to capture power.'[36]

Beside the above special features of Draft Constitution, Dr Ambedkar also discussed in the introduction of his address about the question of 'Constitutional morality', which according to him 'is not a natural sentiment, it has to be cultivated'. He specially added here by saying: 'We must realize that our people have yet to learn it. Democracy in India is only a top-dressing on Indian soil, which is essentially undemocratic.'[37]

At the end Dr Ambedkar before moving into the Draft Constitution, concluded his introductory address by saying:

> No Constitution is perfect and the Drafting Committee itself is suggesting certain amendments to improve the Draft Constitution. But . . . settled by the Drafting Committee is good enough to make in this country a start with. I feel that it is workable, it is flexible and it is strong enough to hold the country together both in peace time and in war time. Indeed, if I may say so, if things go wrong under the new Constitution, the reason will not be that we had a bad Constitution. What we will have to say is that Man was vile. Sir, I move.[38]

Completion of the Constitution

So with the above introductory address of Dr Ambedkar, he moved the Draft Constitution on 4 November 1948 before the Constituent Assembly. The Assembly had three readings. The first reading was in the form of a brief general discussion on the Draft. The second reading began on 15 November 1948 in which the Draft Constitution was discussed clause by clause in detail. The second reading went up to 17 October 1949. For the final and third reading the Constituent Assembly had session from 14 November till 26 November 1949 and after this Constitution was declared passed and it was signed by the President of the Assembly.

During the three readings specially in the second reading, the discussion on various amendments took place. Dr B.R. Ambedkar accepted or rejected various amendments after giving comments. Some of them are referred here as examples. The first reference to the discussion took place on the proposed Article 30 (part IV) dealing with the 'Directive Principles', in which Mr. Mahavir Tyagi proposed to drop the word 'strive' from the sentence which began as 'the State should strive to promote'.[39] But Dr Ambedkar after hearing the various views on this amendment, gave a full explanation why word 'strive' is used in the said Article. In his explanation first he referred to his introductory address and what he said about the 'Directive Principles'. He also reminded the House that:

> [O]ur Constitution as a piece of mechanism lays down what is called parliamentary democracy. By parliamentary democracy we mean 'one man, one vote'. We also mean that every Government should be on the anvil, both in its daily affairs and also at the end of certain period when the voters and the electorate will be given an opportunity to assess the work done by the Government.[40]

Dr Ambedkar made the function of the Directive Principles very clear. He said that these would be the basis of policy of any Government in power which may follow any form of 'economic democracy'. He listed three such forms which included (1) 'individualism', (2) 'socialistic', and (3) the 'communistic'. The Constitution itself does not take any of the position, but lay down the principles in the form of 'Directive Principles' for the people to use for the test of a Government. The word 'strive' according to Dr Ambedkar was very important, it indicated the intention of the Constitution that every Government, whichever ideology it may follow, has to make efforts to implement the Directive Principles as stated in the Constitution. Some explanations are being quoted here to show, how carefully and purposefully each word and expression was used in the Constitution. He said:

> The word 'strive' which occurs in the Draft Constitution, in my judgement, is very important. We have used it because our intention is that even when there are circumstances which prevent the Government, or which stand in the way of the Government giving effect to these Directive Principles, they shall, even under hard and unpropitious circumstances always strive in the fulfillment of these Directives . . . I think my friend Tyagi will see that the word 'strive'

in this context is of great importance and it would be very wrong to delete it.[41]

It is not possible to give many examples of the debates which took place in the Constituent Assembly, because of the length of this chapter and for the purpose of this work. Therefore I will only give one more example of the discussion, from the Assembly Debates. It is concerning the wider sense of the use of word 'minority'..The question was raised for deleting this word from Draft Article 23, clause 1 (presently in Indian Constitution Article 29). The clause 1 began as 'Any section of the citizens in the territory of India or any part . . .' has the right to protect their language, script and culture. Originally in the draft in place 'Any section of the citizen', the expression 'minority' was used and it was altered by the Draft Committee. A question was raised and discussed about this alteration. Again Dr Ambedkar gave a very clear explanation, why this alteration was introduced. He told the House:

> The word is used not merely to indicate the minority in the technical sense, because it was to cover minorities which are not minorities in the technical sense, but which as nonetheless the minorities in the cultural and linguistic sense. For instance, for the purpose of the Article 23, if a certain number of people from Madras came and settled in Bombay for certain purposes, they would be, although not a minority in the technical sense, cultural minorities. . . . The article intends to give protection in the matter of culture, language and script not only to a minority technically but also to a minority in the wider sense of the term, as I have explained just now that is the reason why we dropped the word 'minority'. . . . In order to meet the situation of migration from one province to another, we felt it was described also that such a provision should be incorporated in the Constitution.[42]

The above two examples show the nature and seriousness with which the representatives of the Assembly worked to frame the Constitution of India. The debates in the Assembly continued till 26 November 1949, the day it was passed, adopted and signed by the President of the Assembly.[43] But on 25 November at the close of Assembly session, Dr B.R. Ambedkar gave his closing address as the Chairman of the Drafting Committee. In the address beside thinking and appreciating the contribution of his colleagues, he also made some general observations and some suggestions for the future implementation of the Constitution. Here again very briefly I will sum up Dr Ambedkar's concluding address under the following three sub-heads:

(a) Personal Remarks
(b) Working of the Constitution
(c) Maintaining the Democracy

PERSONAL REMARKS

In response to the recognition and appreciation which Dr Ambedkar received for framing the Constitution of India, he expressed his gratitude in these words:

> As to the compliments that have been showered upon me both by the members of the Assembly as well as by my colleagues of the Drafting Committee I feel so overwhelmed that I cannot find adequate words to express fully my gratitude to them. I came into the Constituent Assembly with no greater aspiration than to safeguard the interests of the Scheduled Castes. I had no remotest idea that I would be called upon to undertake more responsible functions. I was therefore greatly surprised when the Assembly elected me to the Drafting Committee. I was more than surprised when the Drafting Committee elected me to be its Chairman. There were in the Drafting Committee more bigger, better and more competent than myself such as my friend Sir Alladi Krishnaswami Ayyar. I am grateful to the Constituent Assembly and the Drafting Committee for reposing in me so much trust and confidence and to have chosen me as their instrument and given me this opportunity of surviving the country.[44]

Beside offering his thanks the whole Assembly, Dr Ambedkar offered his special thanks to Sir B.N. Ray, the Constitutional

Advisor; S.N. Mukherjee, the Chief Draftsman of the Constitution and members of the staff.

WORKING OF THE CONSTITUTION

About the future working of the Constitution, Dr Ambedkar said in his concluding address that it was going to depend on the people of India and the way their political parties behave. Dr Ambedkar was absolutely sure that the working of the Constitution was going to depend on the people, not on the nature of the Constitution.

> The Constitution can provide only the organs of state such as the Legislature, the Executive and the Judiciary. The factors on which the working of those organs of the State depend are the people and the political parties they will set up as their instruments to carry out their wishes and their politics.

He further added:

> Who can say how the people of India and their parties will behave? Will they uphold Constitutional methods of achieving their purposes or will they prefer revolutionary methods of achieving them? If they adopt the prophet to say that it will fail. It is, therefore, futile to pass any judgement upon the Constitution without reference to the part which the people and their parties are likely to pay.[46]

Dr Ambedkar referred to the criticism to Constitution which came from two groups during the Assembly Debates. He told that the Communist Party criticized, because they wanted the Constitution to be based upon the principle of the Dictatorship of Proletariat. On the other hand the Socialist Party condemned it, because it does not offer them freedom (in case they come to power) to nationalize or socialize all private property without payment of compensation and they also wanted that the Fundamental Rights be absolute in nature without any limitation. So the reasons varied from party to party. Dr B.R. Ambedkar once again emphasized in his concluding address the provision relating to the amendment of the Constitution, because the Indian Constitution as stand today is neither carry on it 'a seal of finality' or 'infallibility'. He also referred to the dual polity as according to which the powers between Centre and States are divided. In this regard he said:

> The basic principle of Federalism is that the Legislative and Executive authority is partitioned between the Centre but by the Constitution itself. . . . The States under our Constitution are no way dependent upon the Centre for their legislative or executive authority. The Centre or the States are co-equal in this matter. It is difficult to see how much a Constitution can be called Centralism. It may be that the Constitution assigns to the Centre too large field for the operation of its legislative and executive authority than is to be found in any other Federal Constitution. It may be that the residuary powers are given to the Centre and not to the States. But these features do not form the essence of federalism.[47]

Dr Ambedkar also while referring to the powers given to Centre at the time of any emergency or war, 'the residual loyalty of the citizen in an emergency must be to the Centre and not to the Constituent States. For it is only the Centre which can work for a common end and for the general interests of the only as a whole.'[48]

MAINTAINING THE DEMOCRACY

By the time Dr Ambedkar completed his observation on the Constitution of Free India, his inner emotions arose to the extent that he came up with some of his reflections on the future of India. He reminded the House on 26 January 1950 that India would be an independent democratic country, but he was worried whether we would retain it or not. He quoted the example, how King Dahar's military commanders accepted the bribes from the agents of Mohammed-bin-Kasim; Jaichand invited Mohammed Ghori to invade India and fight against Prithviraj, some Maratha noblemen and Rajput kings fought on behalf of Mughals, when Shivaji was fighting with Mughal emperors. The same way the British tried to destroy the Sikh rulers, Gulab Singh, their principal commander sat silent and same way when in 1857 a large part of India declared a war of independence against the British, the Sikhs were silent spectators. After giving all these examples he raised a question: 'will history repeat itself?'

Dr Ambedkar emphasized on 26 January 1950 that India would be a democratic country, according to which 'India from that day would have a government of the people, by the people and for the people'. But question again coming to his mind was: 'what would happen to her democratic Constitution? Will she be able to maintain it or will she lose it again?' He said to the House that we must maintain our democracy not merely on form, but also in fact. For maintaining it, he suggested three things.

The first thing, he suggested was to achieve social and economic objectives, we must only use constitutional methods. 'It means' according to him 'we must abandon the bloody methods of revolution. It means that we must abandon the method of civil disobedience, non-cooperation and satyagraha. When there is no way left for constitutional methods for achieving economic and social objective, there was a great deal of justification for unconstitutional methods. But where constitutional methods are open, there can be no justification for these unconstitutional methods.'[49]

The second thing Dr Ambedkar suggested and also by referring to John Stuart Mill, gave a caution, who once said, not 'to lay their liberation at the feet of even a great man, or to trust him with powers, which enables him to subvert their institution'. He further added that such great persons might have rendered greatest service to the country and there is no harm to offer them our thanks, but at all cost 'hero-worship' must be avoided. Dr Ambedkar pointed out that this caution was very necessary for, because we are already have some traditions established in this regard. He said:

> [F]or in India, Bhakti or what may be called the path of devotion or hero-worship, plays a part in its politics unequalled in magnitude by the part it plays in the politics of any other country in the world.

Bhakti in religion may be a road to the salvation of the soul. But in politics, Bhakti or hero-worship is a sure road to degradation and to eventual dictatorship.[50]

The third thing, Dr Ambedkar suggested that we must not content merely with political democracy. The basis of political democracy is 'social democracy'. But what is 'social demo-cracy'? According to Dr Ambedkar it was a way of life, 'which recognises liberty, equality and fraternity on the principle of life'. Three principles of liberty, equality and fraternity have to be taken together, because if we separate them, we 'defeat the very purpose of democracy'. He very powerfully put across his conviction about the future of democracy in these words:

On 26 January 1950, we are going to enter into a life of contradictions. In politics we will have equality and in social and economic life we will have inequality. In politics we will be recognising the principle of one man one vote and one value. In our social and economic life, we shall, by reason of our social and economic structure, continue to deny the principle of one man one value. How long should we continue to live this life of contradiction? How long shall we continue to deny equality in our social and economic life? If we continue to deny it for long, we will do so only by putting our political democracy in peril. We must remove this contradiction at the earliest possible moment or else those who suffer from inequality will blow the structure of political democracy which this Assembly has so laboriously built up.[51]

Dr Ambedkar ended his concluding address with the following challenge not only to the members of the Constituent Assembly, but also to the people of India:

If we wish to preserve the Constitution in which we sought to enshrine the principle of Government of India people, for the people and by the people, let us resolve not to be tardy in the recognition of the evils that lie a cross our path and which include people to prefer Government for the people to Government by the people, nor to be weak in our initiative to remove them. That is the only way to serve the country. I know of no better.[52]

NOTES

1. Constituent Assembly Debates, Official Report, Book No. 5, Lok Sabha Secretariat, New Delhi: 1999, third print, p. 608 (in future references it will be referred as CAD-5).
2. CAD-5, p. 610.
3. Ibid., p. 664.
4. Ibid., p. 754
5. Ibid., p. 788
6. Ibid., p. 828
7. Ibid., p. 890
8. *Dr. Babasaheb Ambedkar: Writings and Speeches*, vol. 13, edited by Vasant Moon, Bombay: Education Department, Government of Maharashtra, 1995, p. v (Foreword).
9. *Dr. Babasaheb Ambedkar: Writings and Speeches*, vol. 10, edited by Vasant Moon, Bombay: Education Department, Government of Maharashtra, 1991, pp. 523–49 (see for detail discussion).
10. *Dr. Babasaheb Ambedkar: Writings and Speeches*, vol. 13, op. cit., pp. 5, 6.
11. Constituent Assembly Debates, Official Report, Book No. 1, Lok Sabha Secretariat, New Delhi: 1999, third print, pp.1, 35 (in future references it will be referred as CAD-1).
12. Ibid., p. 57.
13. Ibid., p. 59.
14. Ibid., pp. 65–70.
15. Ibid., p. 73.
16. Dhananjay Keer: *Dr Ambedkar: Life and Mission*, Bombay: 1992 (reprinted), p. 387.
17. Ibid., 389.
18. See for detail discussion: CAD-1, pp. 99–103.
19. Ibid., p. 100 (top).
20. Ibid., pp. 99–100.
21. Ibid., p. 100 (middle).
22. Ibid., p. 101
23. Ibid., p. 102
24. Ibid., p. 103
25. *Dr Babasaheb Ambedkar*: *Writings and Speeches*, vol. 13, op. cit., pp. 25–6.
26. Ibid., p. 44.

27. Constituent Assembly Debates, Official Report, Book No. 2, Lok Sabha Secretariat, New Delhi: 1999, third print, p. 33 (top) (in future references it will be referred as CAD-2).
28. CAD-2, p. 33 (centre).
29. Ibid., pp. 34–5.
30. Ibid., p. 35.
31. Ibid., p. 36.
32. See for detail discussion CAD-2, pp. 36–7.
33. CAD-2, p. 39.
34. Ibid., p. 40.
35. Ibid., p. 41 (top).
36. Ibid., p. 41 (bottom).
37. Ibid., p. 38.
38. Ibid., p. 44.
39. Ibid., p. 492.
40. Ibid., p. 494.
41. Ibid., p. 495.
42. Ibid., pp. 922–3.
43. CAD-5, p. 995.
44. Ibid., pp. 973–4.
45. Ibid., p. 973.
46. Ibid., p. 975.
47. Ibid., p. 976.
48. Ibid., p. 977.
49. Ibid., p. 978.
50. Ibid., p. 979 (top).
51. Ibid., p. 979 (bottom).
52. Ibid., pp. 980–1.

CHAPTER 6

Vision of a 'Just Society'

One of the key themes of the writings of Bharat Ratna Babasaheb Dr B.R. Ambedkar was the establishment of an 'ideal society'[1] or a 'casteless society'[2] or a society based upon the 'principle of justice'.[3] In his own words, the 'ideal would be a society based on liberty, equality and fraternity'.[4] While giving the meaning of 'justice', he said, 'Justice is simply another name for liberty, equality and fraternity.' Therefore to understand Dr Ambedkar's vision of a 'just society', we have to understand the meaning of these three expressions, i.e. liberty, equality and fraternity. But before that we need to know the context out of which a need for a 'just society' arose. This means we have to understand the existing nature of the Indian society. Dr Ambedkar had a very comprehensive discussion on the existing 'social order' based upon the Hindu classical religion in some of his works, which included 'Philosophy of Hinduism' and 'The Hindu Social Order'. These two works now are part of volume 3 of his writings and speeches.[5] Another point which becomes very clear from Dr Ambedkar's writings is that he was not only a very creative and constructive critic, but also a thinker who came up with alternative proposals also. This is exactly what he did in the case of the existing social order or society. He not only pointed out the evils of the existing social order and ask for a complete change, but also offered an alternative model. This he did in his most well-known work 'Annihilation of Caste'.

An ideal society should be mobile, should be full of channels for conveying a change-taking place in one part to other parts. In an ideal society there should be many interests consciously communicated and shared. There should be varied and free points of contact with other modes of association. In other words there must be social endosmosis.[6]

For the convenience sake, I have divided the discussion in the following three parts:

i. Existing Social Order
ii. An Alternative Society Based Upon Justice
iii. Way to Establish a 'Just Society'

Existing Social Order

According to Dr Ambedkar, the existing social order meant the Hindu social order. But point here which needs attention is that the existing social order was deeply rooted in the Hindu *varna* system. Because of the caste reality, according to Dr B.R. Ambedkar the existing social order does not give any importance to an individual. Therefore in this society an individual does not have any real chance of growth or development as a person. Because of the same reason, the rights of a human being do not find any place in the existing social order.

The unit of Hindu Society (existing Indian Society) is not the individual Brahmin or the individual Kshatriya or the individual Vaishya or the individual Shudra or the individual *Panchama*. Even the family is not regarded by the Hindu social order as the unit of society except for the purposes of marriage and inheritance. The unit of Hindu society is the class or *varna* to use the Hindu technical name for class.[7]

Dr Ambedkar discussed this point, in detail in his essay 'The Hindu Social Order: Its Essential Principles'.[8] According to him the original Hindu social order recognized only four classes or castes, which included Brahmins, Kshatriyas, Vaishyas and Shudras. But these have became five, because *Panchamas* (Untouchables) were added. Because of the above position of the *varna* based social order in it,

[T]here is no room for individual merit and no consideration of individual justice. If the individual has a privilege it is not because it is due to him personally. The privilege goes with the class, and if he is found to enjoy it, it is because he belongs to that class. Contrawise, if an individual is suffering from a wrong, it is not because by his conduct deserves it. The disability is the disability imposed upon the class and if he is found to be labouring under it, it is because he belongs to that class.[9]

Dr Ambedkar to prove his above point, quoted extensively from the Hindu scriptures. He added that because the basis of the above division of classes was divine according to which these 'were created from different parts of the Divine body has generated the belief that it must be divine will that they should remain separate and distinct'.[10]

Dr Ambedkar pointed out that these do not limit up to five divisions only. These get further divided into sub-classes or castes into hundred and thousands. For example, at the time, when he wrote his essay on 'The Hindu Social Order', the total population of all the Brahmins was about a crore and a half, but they were divided into 1886 sub-castes. The same way the other castes were also divided.[11] A study conducted by the Anthropological Survey of India (1993) also proves this. According to it, presently there are about 751 identifiable sub-communities (divisions) of the Dalits alone.[12]

He has listed three basic principles on which the then existing social order stood. The first principle was 'the principle of graded inequality', which was a 'fundamental principle' of this order. As mentioned above, this order not only divided the society horizontally into numerous castes or sub-castes or communities, it badly divided society vertically. According to its given scheme,

[T]he Brahmin is placed at the first in rank. Below him is the Kshatriya. Below the Kshatriya is the Vaishya. Below the Vaishya is the Shudra and below the Shudra is the Ati-Shudra or the Untouchables. This order of precedence among the classes is not merely conventional. It is spiritual, moral and legal. There is no sphere of life which is not regulated by this principle of graded inequality.[13]

The last part of this observation is important, because the principle of graded inequality has been carried into the total human life including social, economic and political.[14]

The second principle which Dr Ambedkar dealt was that of 'fixity of occupations'. According to this principle, the Brahmins were assigned to study and teach, the Kshatriyas were to protect and fight, and the Vaishya was to look after trade and Shudras were assigned to serve. Here the point need to be remembered is that every member of each class had to follow the work assigned to his or her class. There was no scope of individual choice. In fact there were punishments if any member went against this principle.[15]

The third principle was the 'fixation of people within their respective classes'.[16] This means that every person's class status or caste status was decided by birth not by ability.

Before moving to the next section of this chapter, one final point about the existing social order of India is the question, if what Dr Ambedkar said are the things of the past are applicable today also? The answer is affirmative, because a number of official reports of various commissions appointed by the Government of India have endorsed Dr Ambedkar's above position. Two of such reports are referred here. For example, L.M. Shrikant's 'Report of the Commissions for Scheduled Castes and Scheduled Tribes for the Period Ending 31 December, 1951', opened with these words: 'The Caste in Hindu society is still the most powerful factor in determining a man's dignity, calling or profession. Such a rigid caste-system is not found anywhere else outside India.'[17] These words tells us that what Dr Ambedkar said before independence about the existing social order was true even after the independence. Another Commission's report (known as Mandal Commission, made public in 1990), has devoted two full chapters[18] on the same issue. This report says:

> Castes are the building bricks of Hindu social structure. . . . Here we are mainly concerned with the manner in which caste has fragmented the social consciousness of Hindu society by dividing it into numerous groups arranged in hierarchical order. . . . It may be

further remarked that in this process of divisions, groups called castes have been permanently assigned high or low ranks simply on the basis of birth. . . . The social ranks and their respective duties, ordained by God for humanity, were intended to remain fixed and unmovable. Like the limbs of the body, they cannot properly exchange either their place or function.[19]

About the effects of caste system in the Indian society and what change in it has taken place, the report of the Mandal Commission says:

Even if the caste model described by us represents an ideal State, yet it does not negate the fact that caste system has been the most enduring basis of social organization in India or, that, it has divided the Indian society into a large number of hierarchically arranged high and low castes or, that the lower castes have suffered crippling social handicaps for centuries as a result of the low caste status. Similarly, despite all the modifications that caste has undergone over the ages and, specially after Independence, changes in the caste system are representative more of shifts in emphasis than any material alteration in its basic structure.[20]

From the writings of Dr Ambedkar as well as the official reports of various commissions it is clear that the Indian social order is deeply rooted in the *varna* system and because of the rigidity of the caste system practically no 'material alternation in its basic structure' was possible. One of the problems in various efforts has been that very rare attempt has been made to come up with an alternative model of a society. But this not has been the case of Dr Ambedkar, because he was not only suggested the total annihilation of caste or caste based society, but also offered a model of an 'ideal society' or what we call a 'just society'. Both direct and indirect references to his vision of such a society have been made in the previous discussions. Therefore now I will briefly deal as part of the concluding chapter with the Dr Ambedkar's vision of 'An Alternative Society' based upon justice.

An Alternative Society Based Upon Justice

Dr Ambedkar has stated in a number of his writings about the nature of a society, with which he wanted to replace the existing one. For his 'ideal society', he recognized the two essential principles:

> The first is that the individual is an end in himself and that the aim and object of society is the growth of the individual and the development of his personality. Society is not above the individual and if the individual has to subordinate himself to society, it is because such subordination is for his betterment and only to the extent necessary. The second essential is that the terms of associated life between members of society must be regarded by consideration founded on liberty, equality and fraternity.[21]

Here in this observation of Dr Ambedkar, a main point is that in the caste based society, an individual has no place, whereas in his proposed society, individual is the final end. Also in the caste based society a person's relationship with the member of his or her class or with the members of other classes were already fixed, but in Dr Ambedkar envisaged society these relations have to be based on liberty, equality and fraternity. Here the demand on the society is to protect the individual's human rights.

Dr Ambedkar concluded that any good social order or society has also to go through the two tests namely 'the test of justice' and 'the test of utility'. In fact his judgmental analysis of the caste based or Hindu social order was based on these two tests. Beside the two essential principles or tests, one of the most important components was 'justice' or the 'principle of justice', because 'the norm or the criterion for judging right and wrong in the modern society is *justice*'[22] and again 'justice' according to Dr Ambedkar 'is simply another name for liberty, equality and fraternity'.[23] To understand the real nature of the proposed society, we have to know the meaning of liberty, equality and fraternity.

LIBERTY

He has discussed the meaning of 'liberty' in his numerous works. In *Hindu Social Order: Its Essential Principles*, he divided liberty into two categories namely 'civil liberty' and 'political liberty'. The first category, 'civil liberty' according to Dr B.R. Ambedkar refers to the following basic liberties: (1) liberty of movement, which is opposite to arrest without due process of law, (2) liberty of speech, which of course includes liberty of thought, liberty of reading, writing and discussion, and (3) liberty of action. The second category, the 'political liberty', according to Dr Ambedkar 'consists in the right of the individual to share in the framing of laws and in the making and unmaking of governments'.[24] Dr Ambedkar while discussing the meaning of liberty also added that it should be accompanied by three social conditions, which include social equality, economic equality and there must be knowledge (education) made available to all. All these social conditions were restricted to a particular class in the old social order but form an important part in the new social order.[25]

EQUALITY

The general meaning of the expression equality is 'exactly the same or equivalent in measure amount, number, degree, value, or equality'. But the question has been raised if in the literal sense, all the human beings are same. While answering this question, Dr Ambedkar agreed that all the persons may not be equal with regards to 'physical strength, in artistic skill, in material wealth, or mental capacity', but still 'human beings possess, in degree and kind, fundamental characteristics that are common to humanity'. 'The nature and manifestation' of 'the fundamental characteristics', which 'appear in all human beings', are summed up in the phrase 'moral, equality'. Emphasis must be placed on the term 'moral', because 'no rational exponent of moral equality has been disputed'. Therefore 'in essence the phrase "moral equality" asserts in ethical value, a belief to be sustained, and recognition of rights to be respected'. Because 'a society without any respect for human personalities is a band of robbers'.[26]

FRATERNITY

The below are given three statements of Dr Ambedkar which help us in understanding the meaning of 'fraternity', which along with liberty and equality was the cornerstone of an 'ideal' or 'just society'.

1. Dr Ambedkar in 'Philosophy of Hinduism', while talking about a 'just society' said:

There are two forces prevalent in Society, Individualism and Fraternity. Individualism is ever present. Every individual is ever asking 'I and my neighbours, are we all brothers, are we even fiftieth cousins, am I their keeper, why should I do right to them' and under the pressure of his own particular interests acting as though he was an end to himself, thereby developing a non-social and even an anti-social self. Fraternity is a force of opposite character. Fraternity is another name for fellow feeling. It consists in a sentiment which leads an individual to identify himself with the goods of others whereby 'the good of others becomes to him a thing naturally and necessarily to be attended to like any of the physical conditions of our existence'.[27]

2. 'The Hindu Social Order: Its Essential Principles', while discussing 'Fraternity' as one of the key essentials of a 'just society' or what he calls a 'free social order' as compared to the existing Indian caste based social order, says:

Fraternity is the name for the disposition of an individual to treat men as the object of reverence and love and the desire to be in unity with the fellow beings. This statement is well expressed by Paul, when he said 'of one blood are all nations of men. There is neither Jew nor Greek, neither bond nor free, neither male nor female; for yet are all one in Christ Jesus'. Equally well was it expressed when the Pilgrim Fathers on their landing at Plymouth said: 'We are knit together as a body in the most sacred covenant of the Lord . . . by virtue of which we hold ourselves tied to all care of each others' good and of the whole.' These sentiments are of essence of fraternity. Fraternity strengthens socialites and gives to each individual a stronger personal interest in practically consulting the welfare of others.[28]

3. The best summary of Dr Ambedkar's views on fraternity as well as of his 'ideal society' or what we call 'just society', is:

An ideal society should be mobile, should be full of channels for conveying a change taking place in one part to other parts. In an ideal society there should be many interests consciously communicated and shared. There should be varied and free points of contact with other modes of association. In other words there must be social endosmosis. This is fraternity, which is only another name for democracy. Democracy is not merely a form of Government. It is primarily a mode of associated living, of conjoint communicated experience. It is essentially an attitude of respect and reverence towards fellowmen.[29]

Dr Ambedkar's statement is self-explanatory on the meaning of fraternity and his 'ideal society' or his 'alternative society', but then how will this be established?

Way to Establish a 'Just Society'

After reading Dr Ambedkar's main writings, it becomes very clear that he was not just a critic or a person having some new ideas, he was also at the same time a person, who had concrete suggestions for the implementation of the same. For example in his analysis of the existing social order based on the caste, he was very clear what evils it carried, he was also very clear, about 'justice' as the basis of his alternate society. Again at the end regarding how to establish an 'ideal' or 'just society', he was very clear. *Varna* system was the basis of the existing Indian social order and it was this system, which was responsible for all the evils of the existing order. Because of this analysis, he talked about the annihilation of caste. But he was also very clear that it 'is not possible to break caste without annihilating the religious notions on what it, the caste system, is founded'.[30] According to him this was only possible through a *kranti* (revolution), not through a simple reformation. His work on 'Annihilation of Caste' suggested the following way to lay the foundation for the society rooted in justice. He said:

> Whether you do that or you do not, you must give a new doctrinal basis to your Religion–a basis that will be in consonance with Liberty, Equality and Fraternity, in short, with Democracy. I am not authority on the subject. But I am told that for such religious principles as well be in consonance with Liberty, Equality and Fraternity it may not be necessary for you to borrow from foreign sources and that you could draw for such principles on the Upanishads. Whether you could do so without a complete remoulding, a considerable scraping and chipping off the ore they contain, is more than I can say. This means a complete change in the fundamental notions of life. It means a complete change in our look and in attitude towards men and things. It means conversion; but if you do not like the word, I will say, it means new life. But a new life cannot enter a body that is dead. New life can enter only in a new body. The old body must die before a new body can come into existence and a new life can enter into it. To put it simply, the old most cease to be operative before the new can begin to enliven and to pulsate. This is what I meant when I said you must discard the authority of the *Shastras* and destroy the religion of the *Shastras*.[31]

The above statement is the best summary of his suggested methodology of establishing a 'just society'. It does not need any explanation, but still for the sake of further understanding of the same, the following are the three main steps which he suggested to be followed:

I. *New Doctrinal Basis*–Dr Ambedkar suggested the first step to formulate the new doctrinal basis of the Hindu religion, which according to him, has to 'be in consonance with Liberty, Equality and Fraternity'. Here it means to reinterpret part of the scriptures such as Upanishads, which carries the philosophical basis of Hinduism. Dr Ambedkar's stress here was on the radical reinterpretation which involve 'a considerable scraping and chipping off the ore they contain', which presently go against the principle of fraternity or fellow-feeling and does not allow the practice of 'the associated mode of life', which is one of the important basis for the establishment of a 'just society'. Dr Ambedkar in this regard gave the examples of Sikhism and Islam.[32] Because the present doctrinal basis of Hinduism does not fully allow the principles of liberty and equality to be practised, which automatically cancels the people's right of military service, political power to protect them and the right to educate. Dr Ambedkar named three rights as 'physical weapon', 'political weapon' and 'moral weapon', which according to him in the then existing social order was 'denied to the masses in India'.[33] Now to make available these three weapons to the masses was the first step towards the formation of a new social order based upon 'justice'.

II. *A Complete Change in the Fundamental Notions of Life*—The above stated first step, automatically leads to the second by entering into 'the associated mode of life', asking for 'a complete change in the fundamental notions of life'. It means adopting a new set of 'values of life', which in the strict sense is 'conversion' leading to a 'new life'. Again for the establishment of new social order or bringing 'a complete change in the fundamental notions of life', he looked into the following three practical possibilities:

(a) The first action he suggested was to abolish the caste and the various *sub-castes*, because these came into existence only through imitation and excommunication. But he was not fully convinced with this, because he thought the process may stop with the abolition of sub-castes, therefore,
(b) He suggested another action, according to which *inter-caste dining* may be the solution. But again he himself argued against this suggestion. Because there were many castes which allow inter-dining, but it has not succeeded in killing the spirit of caste and the consciousness of caste, therefore,

(c) He suggested another action, which involved *inter-caste marriage*. About this, he said:

> Fusion of blood can alone create the feeling of being kith and kin and unless this feeling of kinship, of being kindred, becomes paramount the separatist feeling, the feeling of being aliens, created by caste will not vanish. Among the Hindu inter-marriage must necessarily be a factor of greater force in social life than it need be in the life of the non-Hindu. Where society is already well-knit by other ties, marriage is an ordinary incident of life. But where society cut as under marriage as a binding force becomes a matter of urgent necessity. *The real remedy for breaking caste is inter-marriage. Nothing else will serve as the solvent of Caste.*[34]

III. *The Old Body Must Die to Receive a New Body*–The second step leading to conversion through a 'u-turn' leading to a new life actually meant going through a death experience, rejecting completely the old life before entering into a new one. This according to Dr Ambedkar was possible if one was willing to 'discard the authority of the *Shastras* and destroy the religion of the *Shastras*'. He strongly suggested: 'You must take the stand that Buddha took. You must take the stand which Guru Nanak took. You must not only discard the *Shastras*, you must deny their authority, as did Buddha and Nanak.'[35] Here point needs to be remembered is that though Lord Buddha and Guru Nanak belonged to a Kshatriya caste and the *Shastras* only allow their caste to study not to teach; yet they both became founder teachers of the two great religions, which means they took the role of Brahmins and through this action rejected the authority of the *Shastras*.

CONCLUSION

Above in three parts, the vision of Dr B.R. Ambedkar's 'just society' based upon the three universal principles namely liberty, equality and fraternity has been discussed. The united name for these principles he used was justice. If one went through the various discussions of Dr Ambedkar very carefully, one definitely will not only understand the meaning of the

Preamble of the Constitution of India, but will also come to know possibly, who was behind the formulation of the Preamble. Dr B.R. Ambedkar indeed was the architect of the Indian Constitution and as a Chairman of the Drafting Committee, he not only introduced the right articles and clauses, but also gave it the right basic structure. The basic structure of the Indian Constitution, its Preamble, has the following four components:

Justice, *social, economic and political;*
Liberty *of thought, expression, belief, faith and worship;*
Equality *of status and of opportunity;*
and to promote among them all
Fraternity *assuring the dignity of the individual and the unity and integrity of the Nation.*[36]

The form of Government envisaged in the Constitution of India and the vision of a 'just society' was same. Of course while giving the meaning of 'fraternity', Dr Ambedkar also said that 'it is only another name of democracy' and about the democracy in his other speech on 'Ranade, Gandhi and Jinnah', he said:

> [D]emocracy was not a form of government: it was essentially a form of society. It may not be necessary for a democratic society to be marked by unity, by community of purpose, by loyalty to public ends and by mutuality of sympathy. But it does unmistakably involve two things. The first is an attitude of mind, an attitude of respect and equality towards their fellows. The second is a social organization free from rigid social barriers.[37]

This statement on 'democracy' makes it very clear that for him there was no difference between a democratic form of Government (particularly, which the Constitution of India upholds) and the alternative society based upon the principle of justice as seen by him. But Dr Ambedkar's envisaged society, it seems is still a thing of the future. Because at the eve of the adoption of the Constitution of India on 25 November 1949, he made the following statement:

We must make our political democracy a social democracy as well. Political democracy cannot last unless there lies at the base of it social democracy. What does social democracy mean? It means a way of life, which recognize liberty, equality and fraternity as the principles of life. These Principles of liberty, equality and fraternity are not to be treated as separate items in a trinity. They form a union of trinity in the sense that to divorce one from the other is to defeat the very purpose of democracy. Liberty can not be divorced from equality, equality cannot be divorced from liberty. Nor can liberty and equality be divorced from fraternity. Without equality, liberty would produce the supremacy of the few over the many. Equality without liberty would kill individual initiating. Without fraternity, liberty and equality could not become a natural course of things. It would require a constable to enforce them. We must begin by acknowledging the fact that there is complete absence of two things in Indian society. One of these equality on the social plane, we have in India a society based on the principle of graded inequality which means elevation for some and degradation for others. On the economic plane, we have a society in which there are some who have immense wealth as against many who live in abject poverty. On 26 January 1950, we are going to enter into a life of contradictions. In politics we will have equality and in social and economic life we will have inequality. In politics we will be recognizing the principle of one man one vote and one vote one value. In our social and economic life, we shall, by reason of our social and economic structure, continue to deny the principle of one man one value. How long shall we continue to live this life of contradictions? How long shall we continue to deny equality in our social and economic life? If we continue to deny it for long, we will do so only by putting our political democracy in peril. We must remove this contradiction at the earliest possible moment or else those who suffer from inequality will blow up the structure of political democracy, which this Assembly has so laboriously built up.[38]

I do not think, Dr Ambedkar's above statement needs further explanation because what he said in 'Annihilation of Caste' or in 'Philosophy of Hinduism' and to the Constituent Assembly on 25 November 1949, is still applicable. The call given by Dr Ambedkar to the nation continues to challenge us to work for the removal of the contradictions of life faced by masses of Indians in their social and economic life, because as long as these contradictions will continue, the 'just society' or 'ideal society' envisaged by him will be the thing of the future.

NOTES

1. B.R. Ambedkar, 'Annihilation of Caste with a Reply to Mahatma Gandhi', in *Dr Babasaheb Ambedkar: Writings and Speeches*, vol. 1, compiled by Vasant Moon, Bombay: Education Department, Government of Maharashtra, 1989, p. 57.
2. Ibid., p. 80.
3. B.R. Ambedkar, 'Philosophy of Hinduism', in *Dr Babasaheb Ambedkar: Writings and Speeches*, vol. 3, compiled by Vasant Moon, Bombay: Education Department., Government of Maharashtra, 1987, p. 25.
4. B.R. Ambedkar, 'Annihilation of Caste', op. cit., p. 57.
5. *Dr Babasaheb Ambedkar: Writings and Speeches*, vol. 3, op. cit., pp. 3–150.
6. B.R. Ambedkar, 'Annihilation of Caste', op. cit., p. 57.
7. B.R. Ambedkar, 'The Hindu Social Order: Its Essential Principles', in *Dr Babasaheb Ambedkar: Writings and Speeches*, vol. 3, op. cit., pp. 99–106.
8. Ibid., p. 99.
9. Ibid., pp. 99–100.
10. Ibid., p. 100.
11. Ibid., p. 102.
12. K.S. Singh: *The Scheduled Castes: People of India*, National Series, vol. II, Delhi, Anthropology Survey of India, 1993, p. 1.
13. B.R. Ambedkar: 'The Hindu Social Order: Its Essential Principles', op. cit., p. 107.
14. Ibid., p. 111. Also see: Reservation for Backward Classes, Mandal Commission Report of the Backward Classes Commission, 1980, (Along with Introduction, Delhi: Akalank Publications, 1990, p. 25) (in future references used as Mandal Commission Report 1980).
15. B.R. Ambedkar, 'The Hindu Social Order: Its Essential Principles', op. cit., pp. 111–13.

16. Ibid., pp. 113–15.
17. L.M. Shrikant, 'Report of the Commission for Scheduled Castes and Scheduled Tribes for the Period Ending 31 December', Delhi: 1951, p. 1.
18. Mandal Commission Report, op. cit., pp. 19–25.
19. Ibid., p. 19.
20. Ibid., p. 23.
21. B.R. Ambedkar, 'The Hindu Social Order: Its Essential Principles', op. cit., p. 95.
22. B.R. Ambedkar, 'Philosophy of Hinduism', op. cit., p. 22.
23. Ibid., p. 25.
24. B.R. Ambedkar, 'The Hindu Social Order: Its Essential Principles', op. cit., p. 98.
25. B.R. Ambedkar, 'Philosophy of Hinduism', op. cit., pp. 38–9.
26. B.R. Ambedkar, 'The Hindu Social Order: Its Essential Principles', op. cit., pp. 96–7.
27. B.R. Ambedkar, 'Philosophy of Hinduism', op. cit., p. 44.
28. B.R. Ambedkar, 'The Hindu Social Order: Its Essential Principles', op. cit., pp. 97–8.
29. B.R. Ambedkar, 'Annihilation of Caste', op. cit., p. 57.
30. Ibid., p. 27.
31. Ibid., pp. 77–8.
32. Ibid., p. 55.
33. Ibid., p. 63.
34. Ibid., p. 67.
35. Ibid., p. 69.
36. P.M. Bakshi: *The Constitution of India with Selective Comments*, Delhi, 1999 (reprint), p. 1.
37. B.R. Ambedkar, 'Ranade, Gandhi and Jinnah', in *Dr Babasaheb Ambedkar: Writings and Speeches*, vol. 1, compiled by Vasant Moon, Bombay: Education Department., Government of Maharashtra, 1989, p. 222.
38. Constituent Assembly Debates, Official Report, Book No. 5, vol. XI, 14–26 November 1949, New Delhi, 1999, third reprint, p. 979.

Index